The THINK Series

THINK about
Foreign Policy

THINK about

Foreign Policy

The U.S. and the World

James A. Cooney

The THINK Series

Walker and Company
720 Fifth Ave.
New York City, NY 10019

List of Illustrations: Foreign Policy

Figures 6, 7, 8, 9, 10, 11, 16 courtesy of the Library of Congress; Figure 13, 14 courtesy of the National Archives; Figures 15, 21 official photo courtesy of the U.S. Air Force; Figure 19 courtesy of the Signal Corps, U.S. Army; Figure 20 courtesy of the National Archives: Nixon Project.

The THINK Series' Editors: William N. Thorndike, Jr., Ramsey R. Walker

Stylistic editor: Martha Goodale, Mary Pavlik
Fact checker: Peter Woodsum
Reading consultants: Anne-Marie Longo, Paula Sable

Jacket design: Joyce C. Weston
Text design: Joyce C. Weston
Photo research: Diane Hamilton
Graphs: Jill Thompson
Jacket illustration: Tom Hughes
Text illustrations: Jeff Danziger
Appendix A written by J. B. Schramm

The editors would like to thank the many teachers, librarians, and students that assisted in putting together the THINK Series. It would be impossible to thank everybody; however, we would especially like to thank the following people: John Buckey, Betty Carter, Jim Davis, Mike Hartoonian, Tedd Levy, David Mallery, Mike Printz, Bill Polk, Ellen Ramsey, Mary Tabor.

Author's Acknowledgements

I have thoroughly enjoyed writing this book. Two major reasons for this are the people with whom I have worked. Will Thorndike has been an ideal editor, skillfully blending an understanding of my work habits with a subtle pressure on me to move ahead with the drafts. Anne Powell has been invaluable in helping me with the manuscript. She understands the tricks of the word processing program better than anyone else and I relied on her advice (based on years of high school teaching experience) to help me decide whether my text was written at the proper level.

Deepest appreciation goes to my two children, Jeffrey and Kimberly, for letting me take over the dining room table and for putting up with all my extra work hours. I hope that they will enjoy reading the book 5–7 years from now.

First published in the United States of America in 1988 by the Walker Publishing Company, Inc.

Published simultaneously in Canada by Thomas Allen & Son Canada, Limited, Markham, Ontario.

Library of Congress Cataloging-in-Publication Data

Cooney, James A.
Think about foreign policy.

(The Think Series)
Bibliography: p.
Includes index.
Summary: Discusses the structure and historical development of foreign policy in the United States and its impact on American citizens.
1. United States—Foreign relations—1945– Juvenile literature. 2. United States—Foreign relations—Juvenile literature. [1. United States—Foreign relations] I. Title. II. Title: The U.S. and the world. III. Series.

E840.C67 1988 327.73 87-21620
ISBN 0-8027-6759-1
ISBN 0-8027-6760-5

Printed in the United States of America

10 9 8 7 6 5 4 3 2 1

CONTENTS

1 What Is American Foreign Policy?

Why has the United States often been reluctant to play an active role in world politics?
How do the President and Congress clash over the making of foreign policy?
Is it possible for American foreign policy to aim for peace in the world while also guaranteeing America's strength?
How do the traditions of U.S. history continue to influence American foreign policy today?

One simple but incomplete answer to this question is that American **foreign policy** is the way the United States chooses to act toward other countries. Which countries does the United States treat as friends? Which countries does the United States protect and how? How does the United States treat "unfriendly" countries? Foreign policy describes the government's actions toward the rest of the world. Understanding American foreign policy means paying attention to all the government's actions in world affairs.

To understand American foreign policy, we have to look at it in relation to American history. The ideas and principles which guided the writers of the Con-

***Figure 1** Foreign policy is the way that the United States chooses to act toward other nations.*

stitution and the Declaration of Independence still influence Americans today. Men like George Washington, Benjamin Franklin, John Adams, John Jay, and Alexander Hamilton wanted the ideas of the American Revolution to affect foreign relations as well as politics within their own country. The genius of the Constitution has been that it can be reinterpreted as times change. Likewise, American foreign policy has changed with the times.

Two hundred years ago America did not worry much about relations with other countries. It was a young nation developing new ideas and a more democratic form of government. Even one hundred years ago the United States still kept itself isolated from the problems of the **Old World** in Europe. American interests were centered on problems at home and on westward expansion on the North American continent. World Wars I and II showed the United States that **isolationism** could no longer succeed. At the end of World War II, America finally assumed its responsibility for global politics. The United States became the "policeman" for the world—or the "big kid on the block." This role is a new one for Americans. Some other countries think the United States still makes some of its mistakes in foreign policy because it is a "young" world power.

The following questions are basic to the understanding of the United States' (or any country's) foreign policy.

1. Who makes foreign policy (which institutions are involved)?
2. How is the policy made (what are the processes)?
3. How much influence does the public have (what are the public attitudes)?

These relationships make foreign policy complicated. The American *institutions,* such as the presidency and the Congress, often clash openly. The *policy-making processes* work very slowly so that everyone's opinion can be heard. The processes are often confusing and conflicting. Some want America's role to be strictly as a peacemaker, while others want America to use its strength to tell other counties how to act. The *attitudes of the people* are sometimes hard to measure, too. In the past, most Americans have not wanted their country to be too active in international affairs, but this is starting to change. When Libya or Iran do something to embarrass or insult the United States, Americans expect a response. Many Americans are also frustrated when the U.S. as a country does not act to protest Soviet actions in Afghanistan or even Japanese trade imbalances with the United States.

Because of these conflicts over the role of institutions, policy-making processes, and people's attitudes, American foreign policy often ends up seeming ineffective and hard to understand. This is not a surprise because there are many conflicting and confusing parts to foreign policy.

The term "American foreign policy" really includes many different kinds of foreign policy. The same is true for American **domestic policy.** Domestic policy describes the programs and ideas that the U.S. government has *within* the country. These domestic policies include housing, social security, agriculture, highways, and many other areas of national concern. When we look at American foreign policy or domestic policy, it is important to ask what does the country want and how can the United States achieve what it wants. Foreign policy is the attempt by a country to reach the goals it sets for itself in the world.

This definition may sound easy to understand but there are two major problems: (1) Everyone in a big country like the United States may not agree about the goals of foreign policy; and (2) even if the goals are clear, America may not reach the goals. The United States may be very upset with Japan because Japan sells so many cars, computers, and stereos to Americans, but American foreign policy cannot force the Japanese to change immediately. American foreign policy also cannot force the Soviets out of Afghanistan, and it cannot guarantee an end to fighting in the Middle East. All that American foreign policy can do is put pressure on other countries and try to convince them to do what America thinks is best. The United States is still learning that it is better to *manage* foreign policy problems over several years than to try to *solve* them immediately.

LOOKING AT FOREIGN POLICY AS A POLITICAL ISSUE

We can see that the picture of American foreign policy reveals some problems. It is easy to have a popular foreign policy when everyone agrees on what should be done and the country has the capability to carry out those goals. Presidents often work hard to convince the American people to accept their strategies. This worked well during World War II, when Hitler's Germany and Imperial Japan were clearly enemies. It also worked well when the United States wanted to respond to the Soviets' success with *Sputnik* in 1957: the American people willingly accepted expensive new programs to catch up with the Soviet space program.

It is difficult to have a popular foreign policy, however, when there is disagreement about what to do, or when the country lacks the power to carry out its policy. During the Vietnam War the country became torn between those who were for and those who were against the war. When Iran held American hostages from November 1, 1979 until January 20, 1981 during President Carter's Administration, many Americans grew frustrated. The United States seemed helpless against the student terrorists. Opposition to U.S. foreign policy can come from inside the country—from Congress, from interest groups, or from the people. Opposition can also come from other countries. Many European friends were upset when American planes bombed Libya in 1986 to try to stop terrorist bomb attacks. The Europeans are also critical of American policy toward South Africa because they feel that the Americans are supporting the South African government's racist policies.

In the early years after World War II, American **allies** seemed to accept American priorities. The United States was clearly the dominant power. These were the golden days of American foreign policy, but gradually the situation changed. As other countries recovered from World War II, they formed their own ideas about foreign policy. The United States was so preoccupied with the Vietnam War in the late 1960s and early 1970s that American allies felt the need to develop their own foreign policies. Now the United States has a more "normal relationship" with other countries. The United States remains a superpower but now must pay more attention to the priorities of American allies when making decisions about foreign policy.

The danger of American foreign policy is that the United States can seem like a "bull in the china shop"—America may be too eager to push its own ideas. Some people accuse the United States of having a "Rambo" foreign policy because the country appears too willing to use military strength (for example, in Central America or in Lebanon in 1983). In the 1950s and 1960s, other countries accused the United States of "Coca-Cola Imperialism," because the U.S. appeared to export American culture (including Coca-Cola) to the whole world.

Historically, the United States has never paid much attention to making foreign policy together with other countries. America expected to formulate its own policy and to have other countries accept it. This was true in both world wars and even until the 1960s. Only in the past twenty years has America recognized that foreign policy has to be discussed with all our allies, even if the United States is stronger militarily and economically than they are.

THE UNIQUE ASPECTS OF AMERICAN FOREIGN POLICY

To understand American foreign policy, we will want to keep three pictures in mind. First, how do American history and traditions affect American foreign policy? For over two hundred years, America has been accustomed to (a) making its own foreign policy, (b) aiming for practical and quick solutions, and (c) serving as a democratic example or model for the rest of the world. It may be difficult to change now.

The second picture involves who makes foreign policy in the United States. What are the institutional arrangements? What does the president do? What do Congress and the State Department do? How do these different institutions interact?

The third picture to look at to understand American foreign policy is how the United States interacts with other countries. Relations with the Soviets are especially critical because the United States and the Soviet Union are the two superpowers. In the early 1970s the Soviets and Americans were on friendly terms, and this affected international relations for the rest of the world. The Europeans, for example, felt that they could make new treaties with the Soviets without upsetting the Americans.

American foreign policy faces a dilemma. The United States is still the most powerful country in the world, but it needs now more than ever before to listen to its allies when making foreign policy. The United States has always felt that international problems can be "solved" permanently if reasonable people will simply talk to one another about finding a solution. According to one American foreign policy expert, foreign policy should be seen as a "mountain range," where the summits and valleys are not in sight and no one can see the next crisis.

But Americans do not like this description. They prefer to see foreign policy as a "flat plain," on which the pilgrims of progress move forward. Foreign policy, in this view, tries to avoid the occasional obstacles or nuisances that might slow down the pilgrims' march. American foreign policy emphasizes solutions. It is designed to be a series of rescue operations to bring the lost traveler back to the plain. The problem is that quick solutions are not always possible. Americans become unhappy very quickly if solutions are not forthcoming. In the past, the United States withdrew from the world's problems, but this is not possible any more.

American foreign policy works best when there is a national consensus on what to do—or, in other words, most of the politicians, government officials, and people in the country are in agreement on what actions are best. This usually happens in a war. It also happened during most of the nineteenth century, when the **Monroe Doctrine** (described in the next chapter) provided a foreign policy which everyone accepted. With the Monroe Doctrine, American foreign policy and the popular will of the people were in tune. The goals of the policy were clear, and people agreed with them. Today, American foreign policy sometimes seems confused because the goals are less obvious and more difficult to attain. The question about which direction American foreign policy should take has been unanswered since the end of the Vietnam War. We will pay special attention to what the possibilities and problems are for the future.

OBJECTIVES

The purpose of this book is to introduce American foreign policy, clarify the ideas behind the policies, and point out the significance of America's role in the world. The goals and objectives of the book are to show that:

- *The people who drafted the Constitution intentionally made it hard for the president and Congress to work together on foreign policy.* In the American system the president, Congress, and the Supreme Court are supposed to share powers. Their powers are separated so that no branch of govenement has too much power. The **separation of powers** was set up deliberately because the writers of the Constitution disliked centralized power. George Washington and the other **founding fathers** knew that the institutions that have responsibility for foreign policy would clash, but the founding fathers did not mind some unpredictability. The competition over who makes foreign policy still continues today. It involves not only the president and Congress but also new actors, such as the State Department, the Department of Defense, and the National Security Council.

- *America has always been unwilling to have a foreign policy.* Only since 1945 has the United States been prepared to accept its role as a major power in international relations. Even now, America often prefers to "do it alone" and make its own policy.

■ *Americans want their foreign policy to bring about peace and guarantee America's strength, a difficult combination.* America wants to be a model democracy for other countries but also a helpful and powerful friend. Other countries sometimes feel that the United States uses too much power—such as in the war against Mexico 140 years ago, the Spanish-American War ninety years ago, the Vietnam War twenty years ago, or even the 1983 invasion of tiny Grenada. The toughest challenge for balancing American peace and security is in America's relationship with the Soviet Union.

***Figure 2** It is often difficult to balance the twin foreign policy goals of strength and peace.*

- *Foreign policy reflects what happens inside American politics.* In other words, domestic politics and foreign politics can be closely related. One of President John F. Kennedy's advisors said that Kennedy was "the first American president for whom the whole world was, in a sense, domestic politics." Oil and other necessary resources are critical for all countries, and American companies may have offices and factories throughout the world.If Iran stops oil tankers in the Persian Gulf, or if Brazil cannot pay money back to international banks for its loans, the United States has to decide how to respond. Commercial relations are part of American foreign policy.

- *American foreign policy changed dramatically after World War II.* After 1945, America finally was willing to stay involved in world politics to guarantee peace, but it is a difficult new role. The United

***Figure 3** The U.S. is dependent on oil from the Middle East and on resources and imports from other countries. This dependence affects foreign policy decisions.*

States is not always certain what kind of foreign policy to use. Should the United States be diplomatic and try to talk with enemy countries, or should military power (including nuclear weapons) be used to force agreement? These problems are most visible in the relationship with the Soviet Union. The Vietnam War was also extremely important for exposing the limits of U.S. foreign policy.

REVIEW QUESTIONS

1. What is the difference between domestic policy and foreign policy?
2. If the American government gives money to farmers, other countries say that that is part of foreign policy. Why?
3. Why do we sometimes say that the United States is the "policeman" for the world? Do you think that this is a good role for the United States?
4. Why can we say that the United States has more "normal" relations with its allies today than in the 1940s or 1950s? Does this make it easier or harder for America to make foreign policy?
5. Why do some people describe American foreign policy with terms such as "a bull in a china shop," "Coca-Cola Imperialism," and "Rambo"?

2 The Structure and History of American Foreign Policy

How does the Constitution set up an "invitation to struggle" between the president and Congress in foreign policy-making?
What power does the president have to make foreign policy?
How was the Monroe Doctrine of 1823 an expression of American isolationism? How did the understanding of the Monroe Doctrine change during the nineteenth century?
What is the relationship between America's policy of isolationism and its desire to serve as a model for the rest of the world?

PART 1: FOREIGN POLICY AND THE CONSTITUTION, THE PRESIDENT, AND THE CONGRESS

American political leaders have always questioned whether or not it was legitimate for the United States to have a foreign policy. This was true two hundred years ago, and it is even true for some politicians today. In the 1920s a senior American military adviser said, "The foreign policy of the United States is to have no foreign policy." The Constitution of the United States reflects some of the uncertainties that the founding fathers had, and these uncertainties still affect the relations between foreign policy actors such as the president and the Congress.

The U.S. Constitution and Foreign Policy

> "The longer I live, the more I am impressed with . . . our American Constitution."
>
> —*President Harry S. Truman*

The writers of the American Constitution in the 18th century wanted to control the power of their rulers and their government. They felt that power could best be controlled by breaking up the power among the political actors. This separation of power guaranteed that the actors would have **checks and balances** on one another. The Constitution gives certain powers to the president for making foreign policy, and it gives other powers to the Congress. Many institutions that influence the making of foreign policy today were not yet established at the time of the drafting of the Constitution. The State Department and the National Security Council are not mentioned, nor are television networks, major newspapers, business corporations, trade unions, or interest groups. But all these actors influence foreign policy.

> "The Constitution . . . is an invitation to struggle for the privilege of directing American foreign policy."
>
> *Edwin S. Corwin* *The President: Office and Powers*

Because of the uncertain relationship among the actors, Corwin claims that the Constitution establishes an open "invitation to struggle." In American history the executive (the president) and the legislative (Congress) branches are always fighting for influence in foreign policy. President George Washington complained loudly when the Senate opposed a treaty with England that he was proposing. At the end of World War I, President Woodrow Wilson was not able to convince the Senate to accept his suggestions for a treaty. From 1837 until 1897, Congress took practically all the initiatives in foreign policy. Congress was also especially powerful in the 1920s and 1930s. In declaring war, however, the Congress almost always accepts the president's decisions. Congress often does not even use its right to question the president's decision. The United States has been involved in eleven major wars in its history, and in only five of those did Congress make a formal declaration of war.

The "invitation to struggle" over foreign policy in the Constitution is easy to recognize:

- The president is commander-in-chief of the armed forces, but Congress has to agree to give the money to pay for these forces.
- The president appoints ambassadors, but the Senate has to confirm them before they can begin work.
- The president may negotiate treaties, but two-thirds of the Senators have to agree to the treaty before it can work.
- Only Congress has the power to "regulate commerce with other nations" and "declare war," but the president can act when necessary.

The president and the Congress have to work together closely, but the Constitution does not explain in detail who has what responsibilities. The Constitution says that the president can make treaties "with the advice and consent of the Senate." President Washington, however, once appeared in person in the Senate to seek advice on a treaty, and the Senators asked him to leave so they could talk in private. After that, Washington never went back for advice. Since then, the Senate has provided "consent" for treaties but not much "advice."

The idea of the Constitution was that it would grow like a tree through the years. New interpretations would be added as the history of the United States unfolded. This flexibility is one reason why the Constitution is often praised as the basis of American government. Difficult areas were simply left open by the writers of the Constitution. These areas are sometimes called the "silences of the Constitution" because they are not addressed. In foreign policy the Constitution has very little to say except about regulating commerce, declaring war, and making a treaty.

Figure 4 The Constitution states that Congress should provide advice and consent to the president on treaties. In practice, Congress provides consent but little advice.

The President and Foreign Policy

Although Congress has tried to be much more involved in foreign policy since the Vietnam War, the fact remains that the president is ultimately in charge. President Truman had a famous sign on his desk that read: "The buck stops here," meaning that the president is the person responsible for the final decision. In foreign policy that is certainly true. The Constitution also aimed to limit the president's power to "make war" because the writers of the Constitution did not want the president to have as much power as the British king had had. But over the years presidents have gained more power in foreign policy, not less.

- In 1817 President James Madison waited one whole year before sending the nation's first arms control treaty, the Rush-Bagot Treaty, to the Senate.
- President James Monroe ignored Congress in 1823 when he announced the Monroe Doctrine, the most important idea in American foreign policy in the nineteenth century.
- In 1940 President Franklin Roosevelt reversed twenty years of American isolationism when he gave fifty old ships to the British to use for the war against Germany. The exchange of the ships for the right to use British naval bases in the Atlantic was made through a simple exchange of notes, so again Congress was not involved.
- When President Truman sent troops to Korea in the early 1950s, and when President Lyndon Johnson sent half a million troops to Vietnam in the mid-1960s, neither called the American actions a

war. Congress, therefore, was never even asked to declare war.

- President Richard Nixon did not ask Congress for approval when he extended the Vietnam War into Laos and Cambodia in the 1970s.

Within the American government system, the president is quite strong. He is probably stronger than the men who wrote the Constitution expected him to be, and he is stronger than many congresspersons would like. Compared to other nations, however, the power of the presidency often seems weak. Dictators can simply announce their foreign policy. Even in other democracies the leaders often are more able to state their policy without all the "checks and balances" that the American system has. The weakness of the president has been evident for a long time.

- After World War I, in 1919, President Wilson was not able to convince the U.S. to join the **League of Nations.**
- President Franklin Roosevelt could not enter into an alliance with England, which was engaged in a war with Germany in 1939–40.
- In 1976 President Gerald Ford was unable to make a secret intervention against Communist rebels in Angola.
- In 1978 President Jimmy Carter barely convinced the Senate to give control of the Canal Zone back to Panama.

The power of the presidency depends on the person in office and on the situation. Remember that the president heads the executive branch of the government, but there are other important parts of the executive branch that also make foreign policy. The State Department, the Defense Department, the Central Intelligence Agency, and the National Security Agency all help to make the president stronger. Congress passed the **National Security Act of 1947** to strengthen the president's hand in foreign policy. Congress recognized that if the United States wanted to play a more active role in international relations, then the executive branch would have to be reorganized to make it stronger. The National Security Act of 1947 established:

- a significantly larger Department of State;
- a new Department of Defense, which combined the old War Department and the Department of the Navy;
- a Central Intelligence Agency (CIA), which was designed to coordinate American efforts to collect intelligence about other countries;
- a new National Security Council that serves the president directly and is supposed to help him coordinate all the foreign policy recommendations that he receives, from the departments of State and Defense, for example.

Some presidents have had a remarkable influence on foreign policy. James Polk and William McKinley pushed America into wars with Mexico and Spain in the nineteenth century. Woodrow Wilson's dream was to cure the world of war after World War I. Franklin Roosevelt brought America back into the center stage of international politics in 1940, after American policy had virtually ignored the rest of the world for twenty years. Other presidents were more content to leave the running of foreign policy to the

secretary of state. Abraham Lincoln, Ulysses Grant, Warren G. Harding, and Calvin Coolidge are examples of presidents who were not particularly interested in foreign policy.

This balance between strong presidents and strong secretaries of state has continued in the post-war era. Some presidents have left responsibility to their secretaries of state. Other presidents have relied on the **national security adviser.** The White House was dominant in foreign policy under President John Kennedy and National Security Adviser McGeorge Bundy and also under President Nixon and National Security Adviser Henry Kissinger. The secretaries of state who provided leadership were George Marshall and Dean Acheson under President Truman, John Foster Dulles under President Dwight Eisenhower, and Henry Kissinger under President Gerald Ford.

Sometimes there is a conflict between the secretary of state and the national security adviser. The secretary of state has the advantage of thousands of employees working for him in the State Department, but the national security adviser has the advantage of being free from bureaucracy and being able to see the president often and informally.

The number of people who specialize in foreign policy in the executive branch has grown enormously since World War II. (The executive branch consists of the president and all the departments that work for him, such as the State Department and the Department of Defense.) In some ways this giant bureaucracy helps the president make decisions about foreign policy because he has so many experts available. In other ways, though, the bureaucracy slows down the foreign policy process because so many departments, agencies, and bureaus are involved in every decision. There are bound to be different opinions. When President Carter considered using a new kind of nuclear weapon in Europe—the neutron bomb—the State Department said it was a bad idea because of the antinuclear feelings in Europe. The Defense Department, however, said that it was a good idea to start putting the weapons in place immediately. The Defense Department thought in military terms and was not as interested in the opinions of the Europeans who lived in the countries where the bombs would be located, whereas the State Department was not as interested in military needs.

The power of the president can be enormous in crisis situations when everyone recognizes the need to let the president act. In most situations, however, the power of the presidency is limited because the president must steer a fine line between many institutions and interest groups. The president cannot simply tell everyone what to do in government. He has to convince them to follow his recommendations. President Truman complained about this when he said, "I sit here all day trying to persuade people to do the things that they ought to have sense enough to do without my persuading them. . . . That's all the powers of the President amount to." The main power that the president has is to *persuade* others to accept his policies. He has to bargain with the other actors.

An example of the president failing to persuade occurred in the early 1960s. During the Cuban Missile Crisis, President Kennedy was engaged in life-and-death negotiations about the Soviet missiles in Cuba. The U.S. Ambassador to the United Nations suggested that the United States offer to remove some old missiles in Turkey in return for the Soviet removal of their missiles in Cuba. The president said that no trade was possible because he had ordered those missiles removed from Turkey several months earlier. Someone had to tell the president that *no one had carried out his order*. The missiles were still in Turkey. Even when the president says he wants something done, that does not guarantee that it will be done.

Congress and Foreign Policy

Congress and the president are partners in making foreign policy, but the Congress generally accepts the idea that the president should control foreign policy. Although Congress feels that the president should be responsible for the initiatives in foreign policy, Congress is always ready to challenge the president on his policies. Many Congresspersons have served on committees for years and years and therefore have become experts in certain areas. They may even know more about a subject than a new top-level government appointee who is just beginning a job.

Congress has some ability to control the president because it can make investigations and use confirmation hearings to examine people whom the president is appointing to office. Congress investigated Watergate and uncovered important information. The investigation reminded the public how important it is for Congress to oversee what the president does.

In regard to foreign policy, the formal powers of Congress are mainly to "make war" and "regulate commerce with foreign nations." This last power was critical to the founding fathers because they saw commercial powers as more important than political powers. The main way Congress checks the power of the president is through the "purse strings"—Congress can refuse to give the president the money he needs for programs. Congress can also stop the president from giving money to certain countries. The president often feels that Congress is getting in his way with these limits, but he has to accept them.

Presidents have to learn to cooperate with Congress. Woodrow Wilson failed to do this with his plans for peace after World War I, and Congress rejected his ideas. Franklin Roosevelt saw Wilson's mistake. Even with all the wartime powers that he was given by Congress, Roosevelt was careful in World War II to work closely with the members of Congress. Roosevelt and every other American president in the last forty years knew that Congress can make it very difficult for the president to carry out his foreign policy if Congress is angry with him. Wilson had not included Congress in his planning for the League of Nations. To avoid this same situation, Roosevelt asked many members of Congress from both parties to help him make plans for the United Nations in 1945.

The role that Congress plays in foreign policy changes depending on the kind of decision that needs to be made. Foreign policy decisions can be (1) crisis decisions, (2) decisions to declare an existing policy change, which does not need additional funding or a change in American obligations, or (3) more significant policy decisions. The president plays the most important role in the first two kinds of decisions.

If there is a crisis, Congress is usually willing to let the president be in charge. Congress is not able to react with the speed, secrecy, and unified purpose that a crisis demands. In the Cuban Missile Crisis, President Kennedy had to act very quickly. He only talked with his closest advisers, but Congress accepted his decisions. The president is also the key actor when small changes are made in policy that already exists.

For example, **NATO** (North Atlantic Treaty Organization) is the military alliance between America and its allies in Europe. NATO was formed in 1949. In 1963 the European allies wanted to form a "NATO nuclear force" with the United States. This force would allow the Europeans to share responsibility for using nuclear weapons in Europe. President Kennedy did not ask Congress about this. He simply announced his decision. No new costs or troops were needed, and the president still had the final word about using nuclear weapons.

With more significant policy decisions, however, Congress can have more influence. A different kind of national policy decision is necessary. New resources or a new consensus may be needed. Congress may have to agree to give more money for a program or it may have to approve a new treaty. If the president had wanted soldiers from several NATO countries to share control of the nuclear weapons, he would have needed approval from Congress. American laws do not allow nuclear weapons to be used unless the president makes the decision. To share control of the weapons with other countries would be illegal. In these kinds of decisions, Congress still can play a significant role.

Congress also has the power to put important limits on what a president can do. In 1973 Congress was upset with the way in which Presidents Johnson and Nixon had carried on the war in Vietnam without consulting Congress. Congress passed the *War Powers Act* to make sure that presidents had to pay more attention to Congress in the future. The president is now required to do the following:

- *consult Congress before sending U.S. troops into any fighting (unless America is directly attacked—then the president can act without checking with Congress);*
- *report to Congress within forty eight hours after the troops are sent;*
- *withdraw forces in sixty days unless Congress agrees that the troops can stay.*

The War Powers Act was passed when the reputation of the president was very low. People were upset about the war in Vietnam; they were hearing about illegal CIA activities in the United States, which the White House had allowed; and the Watergate controversy was in the newspaper headlines every day. Without those conditions, the War Powers Act might not have passed. It is not clear how effective this legislation will actually be.

In a long war, Congress still has to approve the money for the war each year, and Congress is hesitant to disagree with the president. From 1966 to 1973 Congress took 113 votes to end or limit America's role in Vietnam. Almost all the votes failed; the only ones that passed and became law were not important. The War Powers Act is a reminder, though, that the president can only push the Congress so far. The president cannot afford to ignore Congress.

In 1978 President Carter wanted Congress to ratify (agree to) the Panama Canal Treaty. Careful negotiations had gone on for thirteen years, but suddenly every senator seemed to want to "improve" the treaty. The president had to negotiate with each senator. Over forty U.S. Senators visited Panama for talks with the Panamanian leadership. Congress could not control its own members. The president had to struggle to get the necessary votes.

Perhaps President Carter would not have had so many problems if his relations with the Senate leadership had been better, but the Panama Treaty problems shows that the opinions in Congress can be very divided. Sometimes it is very hard to discover what Congress thinks about an issue. Presidents, of course, feel that this is another reason why foreign policy leadership should rest mainly in the White House.

In conclusion, the best role for Congress in foreign policy is to set broad limits on what the president can do. Congress is not good at making specific foreign policy because there are 535 very independent politicians sitting in the Senate and the House of Representatives. That makes it almost impossible for Congress to suggest initiatives in foreign policy, especially in a crisis. But Congress can cripple the president's foreign policy very easily when there is disagreement between the two branches.

Congress is not designed to play the major role in foreign policy. The Congresspersons have to think constantly about being reelected. Foreign policy decisions do not win votes at home. Because Congresspersons would rather give money to their own districts they have always been very willing to cut American financial help to other countries. Congress leaves it to the president to ask for foreign aid and protect America's reputation for generosity with other countries.

The Supreme Court has the opportunity to be another "check and balance" on the White House, but it has not done this in foreign policy. The Supreme Court has left the president very free to carry out foreign policy. For example, the Court refused to rule against the decisions of Presidents Johnson and Nixon to wage war in Vietnam.

The Supreme Court did not rule against the remarkable steps that Abraham Lincoln took during the Civil War. After Fort Sumter was attacked, Lincoln stopped Congress from opening for ten weeks while he built up his army and navy beyond permitted limits, spent money that Congress had not given him, censored the mail, and blockaded the Confederacy. Lincoln went so far in taking these powers that no other president has used his steps as an example.

Congress has developed powers in areas of foreign policy not mentioned by the Constitution. Congress is responsible for laws concerning immigration, the rights of aliens in the United States, and diplomatic immunity. Also, Congress can acquire territory for the United States if the House and Senate agree on a joint resolution.

In daily negotiations about foreign policy, however, Congress is not as effective as the president. It is better for Congress to leave the president freedom in these day-to-day decisions. Congress and the president work best together when they cooperate. For example, since the 1970s the president has had to report carefully to the Congress on secret American intelligence operations in foreign countries. He also has to inform eight different committees in Congress if he is using U.S. troops abroad. In this way, Congress *oversees* decisions made by the White House. This is an important safeguard in the implementation of American foreign policy.

PART 2: THE HISTORICAL DEVELOPMENT OF FOREIGN POLICY

Colonial Views about U.S. Foreign Policy

During peace negotiations with Great Britain in 1782, John Adams, who later became president, told the British negotiators that he was afraid of the European countries. He said "It is obvious that all the powers of Europe will be continually maneuvering with us, to work us into their real or imaginary balances of power." For the next 150 years, this belief was probably the most important idea in American foreign policy. America had won its independence from the Old World in Europe, and now the American republic should have as little contact as possible with the Old

Figure 5 Congress watching over the White House. One job of Congress in foreign policy is to monitor the activities of the president and the executive branch.

World. The American expectation was that if the United States did not interfere in European affairs, then the European powers would leave America alone. America had an isolationist foreign policy, and this idea of doing everything alone did not begin to disappear until after World War II.

For two reasons, though, the United States was not completely isolationist. First, it would have been too risky for America's security if the country had remained neutral with all the European powers. Benjamin Franklin accepted an alliance with France after the Revolutionary War because he wanted protection against the British forts on America's borders. Second, the United States wanted to serve as an example for other countries struggling to become free. This too might have required some international involvement.

America had two conflicting goals: America wanted to be free from outside influences, but at the same time it wanted to be a model for other countries trying to win freedom. When two ideas or goals conflict, it is called a paradox—and American foreign policy has always faced this paradox. Should America have an isolationist foreign policy, or should America try to be very active in foreign policy and set an example for others?

In the early years of the American government,an isolationist foreign policy was emphasized. This made sense because the United States needed time to understand how its new government would work. George Washington was one of the strongest supporters of an isolationist foreign policy. **Washington's Farewell Address** in 1796 is one of the most famous statements of this belief.

Washington's Farewell Address

> . . . foreign influence is one of the most baneful foes of republican government. . . . The great rule of conduct for us in regard to foreign nations is, in extending our commercial relations to have with them as little *political* connection as possible. . . . Our detached and distant situation invites and enables us to pursue a different course. . . . It is our true policy to steer clear of permanent alliances with any portion of the foreign world. . . . There can be no greater error than to expect or calculate upon real favors from nation to nation.

Note, though, that George Washington never said that the United States should give up its freedom of choice to make foreign policy decisions. He also never said that America could not protect itself or defend its interests. Washington recognized that sometimes America might even need "temporary alliances for extraordinary purposes." The key point for Washington was that the United States should not be too committed to one country or one alliance. This idea was accepted by American foreign policy-makers until after 1945, but now there is a very different view about alliances. In the past forty years the United States has seen alliances as necessary for our national security.

The Constitution assumed that the president would need some "executive departments" to assist him with his responsibilities, but the Constitution does not mention any specific departments. In mid-1789, therefore, Congress set up the Departments of Foreign Affairs, War, and Treasury. The Department of Foreign Affairs was supposed to be the strongest department.

Why do we say Department of State rather than Department of Foreign Affairs? Six weeks after Congress established the Departments of Foreign Affairs, War and Treasury, it realized that many duties of government did not fit the description of any of the three departments. The government had to publish federal laws, print money, issue patents, take care of immigration issues, copyright books and maps, publish census returns, control immigration, issue commercial reports, and save the records of the president. This all fell to the Department of Foreign Affairs. Since these duties were not part of foreign affairs, Congress changed the name to the Department of State.

The first official secretary of state under the Constitution was Thomas Jefferson, who took office in 1790. The first Department for Foreign Affairs established by Congress had only six employees in Washington. Benjamin Franklin was one of the first American diplomats. In Paris he liked to have the image of a poor Quaker and a backwoods philosopher, but actually he was one of the richest men in America.

The State Department did not grow significantly until the twentieth century. Even in the 1920s the United States had only twenty ambassadors. The State Department today has over six thousand people working for it in Washington and thousands more in nearly three hundred embassies and consulates around the world.

The first years of American foreign policy were marked by the question of whether to remain distant from world affairs or to be active while spreading the

***Figure 6** President Washington with the first cabinet (from left to right, Knox, Jefferson, Randolph, Hamilton, and Washington).*

ideas of the American Revolution. Even George Washington, who clearly wanted the United States to be independent from European politics, recognized that sometimes America had to consider more involvement. He said that it was America's duty to preserve the "sacred fire of liberty and the destiny of the Republican model of Government." These early views on American foreign policy—the balance between isolationism and active involvement in international affairs combined with the desire of the founding fathers to have decentralized power in the government—still are important for understanding American foreign policies in the 1980s.

The Monroe Doctrine and Nineteenth-Century Policy

Throughout the nineteenth century, the main theme of American foreign policy was isolationism, but Americans also felt that their country had a special mission. This mission was to defend and promote democracy. In 1823 President Monroe declared the *Monroe Doctrine*. This policy was popular with the American people, and it signaled America's readiness to defend its own interests.

The Monroe Doctrine announced that the United States would protect the Western Hemisphere (the Western Hemisphere is North and South America) from any European attacks. America told Europe not to look for any colonies in America's own backyard. In other words, America was saying, "Leave us alone and leave the other countries in the Western Hemisphere alone, too." The message to Europe (especially to Spain, which looked longingly at South America where it wanted to reestablish colonies, and to Russia, which looked at the northwest coast of

North America) was that Europe's power ended at the water's edge.

The Monroe Doctrine was delivered in a message to Congress December 2, 1823, and it said: ". . . the American continents, by the free and independent condition which they have assumed and maintain, are henceforth not to be considered as subjects for future colonization by any European powers."

President Monroe let the European powers know that any effort by them to control or oppose governments in the Western Hemisphere would be viewed in America "as the manifestation of an unfriendly disposition towards the United States." America was announcing a clear foreign policy that took isolationism one step further and said that the United States

Figure 7 President Monroe, standing, discusses the Monroe Doctrine with his advisors.

would protect other countries in North and South America from European interference.

The Monroe Doctrine and American "Spheres of Influence": Some people who criticize the Monroe Doctrine see a conflict between the message to the Europeans and the special mission reserved for the United States of defending and promoting democracy. America told the European powers to leave the countries in the western Hemisphere alone. There could be no more colonies. But America also said that it had a special interest in these countries. The United States, in some ways, declared a "sphere of influence" for itself. Some Europeans felt that America was looking for its own colonies. The Europeans saw a conflict between saying "stay away" to the Europeans and reserving special influence for the United States. This debate is relevant today for American policy in Central America. The United States, for example, still wants to minimize the influence of the Soviet Union in the Westen Hemisphere. America feels that the Soviets have too much influence in El Salvador and Nicaragua.

The Monroe Doctrine expressed a new political self-awareness in America. This was a statement about the defense of the United States: Americans would stand up to other countries to preserve American ideas and values. President Monroe said that he based the doctrine on "our peace and security." The ideas behind the Monroe Doctrine were popular with the American people, and support for the ideas grew throughout the nineteenth century.

When Monroe announced his ideas, he did it in a simple message to Congress, and he never said anything about a "doctrine." A doctrine usually means a fixed idea or a rule. The Monroe Doctrine, however, was a set of ideas which evolved over time and ended up being one of the most important concepts in the history of American foreign policy.

It is important to note that the Monroe Doctrine said nothing about using American troops to support it. President Monroe made it clear that decisions about a military response would have to come from Congress. In fact, the United States lacked the power to back up the Monroe Doctrine, but the British Royal Navy put the "teeth" into the policy. Britain shared America's interst in stopping the other European countries from establishing more colonies in the New World. The British Navy protected both oceans.

The language of the Monroe Doctrine did not define a clear and decisive policy from the start. No one even called this national policy the "Monroe Doctrine" until twenty years after it was presented. But the popularity of the policy grew because it combined the wishes of the American people to develop without outside interference and to allow other countries to develop that way, too. In the next few decades the United States went throught its own *expansionism.* The boundaries of the country were pushed in all directions, and the Monroe Doctrine was often cited as the justification.

- *In the 1840s President James Polk asserted the Doctrine with regard to Oregon, California, and Texas.*
- *In the 1860s Emperor Napoleon III tried to set up a monarchy in Mexico under a prince from Austria. American objections based on the Monroe Doctrine contributed to the failure of this attempt.*
- *President Ulysses Grant used the Doctrine to say that*

America should be involved when a territory in the Western Hemisphere was transferred from one European power to another.

- *President Rutherford Hayes linked the Doctrine to American opposition to a canal between the Atlantic and Pacific oceans, which was controlled by a European country.*
- *President Grover Cleveland insisted that the Doctrine allowed the United States to be the negotiator in any controversy between European and American states.*

The Monroe Doctrine was an extension of George Washington's Farewell Address. Washington supported the idea of American isolationism. The Monroe Doctrine carried Washington's idea one step further and claimed that the entire Western Hemisphere fit into the American "sphere of influence" and therefore should be able to develop without any more European interference. By the end of the nineteenth century, the United States was without doubt one of the most powerful countries in the world. America was willing to have a more active foreign policy, but it was still based largely on the Monroe Doctrine.

The Spanish-American War

In 1898 America won a stunning victory over Spain in just three months. Many people said that America became a great power overnight because of this victory, but the seeds of America's power were already planted after the Civil War. The United States had agricultural and industrial power, a growing population, a trained army and navy from the Civil War, and a modern transportation system.

Why did America fight the **Spanish-American War?**

There were several reasons. Americans wanted to free Cuba from Spain. They believed that the Spanish were treating the Cubans terribly. The newspapers contributed to the "war fever." The headlines screamed about the need for war. When a correspondent for a major New York newspaper reported that nothing was happening in Cuba, the editor sent back a telegram saying, "You furnish the pictures and I'll furnish the war." This was called "yellow journalism" because some editors wanted to create a war to sell more newspapers. The headlines cried out, "Massacre!" or "Bodies Thrown into Trenches and Left Unburied!" When the American battleship USS *Maine* blew up in the harbor of Havana, Cuba, killing 260 Americans, the newspapers demanded war against Spain. It turned out that the Spanish were not responsible for the explosion, but the American public still wanted war.

That was the main reason for the war: The American people wanted it. Presidents Cleveland and McKinley resisted the war, but they were swept along by public opinion and by Congress. It is remarkable that they could postpone the war until 1898, because the American people were calling for war three years earlier. In many ways, the war had more to do with what was happening in American domestic politics than with any argument with Spain.

After the Civil War ended in 1865, life changed dramatically for the American people. As the country went through the "Industrial Revolution," the old life that people had known disappeared. Many farmers lost their land and workers lost their jobs because of the economic problems of the 1890s. Even the middle-class people felt uncomfortable with the new life in

Figure 8 A cartoon shows a Spanish beast surrounded by "mutilated" American soldiers. Anti-Spanish "yellow journalism" led directly to American involvement in the Spanish-American War.

the cities. A war with Spain was the perfect solution for American domestic tensions because (1) Spain was unpopular in the United States and (2) the Americans felt good about what they were doing since they were helping to free the Cubans. The war was described as a "splendid little war," and Theodore Roosevelt, one of the heroes of the war, said: "It wasn't much of a war, but it was the best we had."

For Americans the war was a chance to show their old values. It was a return to the simple life they had led before. Americans did not think of the war as a fight between a strong United States and a weak Spain. The people felt that the war was a victory for the tradition of individualism, which America had always represented. The enemy, Spain, represented centralized government. The American army did not fight against Spain. Instead, the U.S. forces were made up primarily of small army units of volunteers from each of the states, with a scattering of U.S. Army regulars. These small units believed in the "power of individual initiative." Teddy Roosevelt's **Rough Riders** were the most famous unit. Actually, the units were poorly organized, and they probably would have lost the war except that the Spanish army was more incompetent. For Americans, though, the victory showed that small-town America could triumph over the centralizing forces of the Industrial Revolution.

The war with Spain fit in with the aims of American foreign policy during the last twenty years of the nineteenth century. Three themes were typical for America's rise to power in these years. The United States wanted to do the following:

- *become an economic power;*
- *extend its political influence beyond U.S. borders;*
- *carry out America's mission to bring democracy to the rest of the world.*

In other words, America had been so successful with its economic production that it needed new overseas markets for its extra goods. As America had success expanding its economic influence, many people decided that they wanted to expand American political influence, too. The Spanish-American War was one way to do this. The main way that America tried to increase its political influence was to encourage democracy and republican ideals around the world.

The new economic and social conditions that swept across America in the late nineteenth century were hard on many people. The war with Spain let people eliminate some of their frustrations and also celebrate the old values of individualism and small-town America. People wanted a return to a familiar and less threatening way of life. In short, the problems in everyday American life had a big effect on the nation's foreign policy.

The Spanish-American War also represented a significant addition to the interpretation of the Monroe Doctrine. President Theodore Roosevelt took the doctrine another step when he said that sometimes the United States might need to act as a policeman in its own Western Hemisphere and might have to intervene in its own sphere of influence. As Roosevelt said,

> Chronic wrongdoing . . . may in America, as elsewhere, ultimately require intervention by some civilized nation, and in the Western Hemisphere the

***Figure 9** President Theodore Roosevelt, big stick in hand, as policeman of the world, California 1905.*

> adherence of the United States to the Monroe Doctrine may force the United States . . . to the exercise of an international police power.

This certainly was a new and broad understanding of the Monroe Doctrine, but it fit into Roosevelt's ideas about foreign policy. Roosevelt did not like the idea of isolationism. He wanted American foreign policy to be more active.

America and the League of Nations

President Woodrow Wilson had a very different problem after World War I. Wilson wanted the United States to play an important role in the League of Nations, an international association of countries whose purposes was to prevent future war. The League was Wilson's idea to make sure that there would be no more terrible wars like World War I.

The American people and the U.S. Senate, however, gave a strong "no" to Wilson's plans. What happened? After the Spanish-American War in 1898, it looked as if America would have an active foreign policy. Twenty years later, after World War I ended in 1918, America wanted no involvement in foreign affairs. How can the change be explained?

World War I started in 1914 in Europe, but the United States did not enter the war until 1917. No one really wanted the war in Europe, but the countries were all tied together by alliances (promises to help each other in case of war). The United States had always avoided alliances, and therefore America was not automatically pulled into this "Great War" (as it was called up until 1931 when World War II began).

President Wilson was reelected in 1916 with the slogan, "He kept us out of war." America tried to remain neutral, but once it entered the war the United States wanted to discover a solution so that such wars would never happen again. That was Wilson's fondest hope. The president tried to convince the American people and the European leaders that his vision of the future should be accepted.

Wilson felt that the **"balance of power" system** had led to the war. The balance of power system meant that countries joined together in alliances to protect themselves from their enemies. At the start of the war, Britain, France, and Russia belonged to one alliance; Germany, Austria-Hungary, and Italy belonged to the other (Italy switched sides one year later). Wilson wanted to replace the balance of power system with a system in which all the powerful countries tried to work together to keep peace. Wilson's system was called **collective security.** Wilson declared, "There must not be a balance of power but a community of power. . . . When all unite to act in the same sense and with the same purpose, all act in the common interest and are free to live their own lives under a common protection."

In some ways, Wilson's ideas were similar to the ideas of the founding fathers: America should avoid entangling alliances in Europe. On the other hand, Wilson was ready to have the United States remain active in world politics. This represented a dramatic change in U.S. foreign policy. Was the country ready for this change? The big debate in the country after World War I was between Wilson and his opponents in the Senate, who did not want as much international involvement for America. The two positions can be seen in the following quotes:

> Our isolation was ended 20 years ago. . . . There can be no question of our ceasing to be a world power. The only question is whether we can refuse the moral leadership that is offered us, whether we shall accept or reject the confidence of the world.
>
> —*Woodrow Wilson, 1919*

> There is a wide difference between taking a suitable part and bearing a due responsibility in world affairs and plunging the United States into every controversy and conflict on the face of the globe. By meddling in

> all the differences which may arise among any portion or fragment of humankind we simply fritter away our influence and injure ourselves to no good purpose.
>
> —*Senator Henry Cabot Lodge, 1919*

This debate between the president and the Senate was probably the most important American debate since the one about the Constitution that lasted from 1787–89. The issue was what kind of foreign policy America should have.

The president said that the world was almost crying out for American leadership. Senator Lodge and the other opponents in the Senate were more cautious about how involved America should be in international events. They worried that America would lose its influence if it became too active. It would be unfair to say that Wilson's opponents were simply isolationists. Many were in favor of American involement internationally, but on a more limited basis than Wilson urged. They were very worried that the president's collective security idea would commit the United States to be a referee in too many international arguments.

Ten months before the end of World War I, Wilson announced a peace program. The plan was called the **Fourteen Points,** and the most important point suggested a "League of Nations" with all the world's nations as members. The League would guarantee peace and independence in the world.

Two months after the war, Wilson traveled to France to attend the Paris Peace Conference at Versailles. He wanted to convince the European allies to use his Fourteen Points as a guide for the peace treaty. The European people welcomed Wilson as a hero, but their leaders were very skeptical about the president's plans. The European leaders thought that Wilson was too idealistic and that he did not understand the reality of European politics. The British prime minister campaigned for reelection by arguing, "Hang the kaiser (the German emperor) and make the Germans pay the cost of the war!" The French premier made fun of Wilson's Fourteen Points by saying that Wilson claimed four more points than the Lord Himself. The French premier also shocked the Americans when he said that his guiding light at the peace conference would be the old balance of power idea.

In short, President Wilson faced a difficult challenge at the Paris Peace Conference. To achieve his main goal—the League of Nations—the president compromised on most of his other Fourteen Points. He had to give in on his hopes for freedom of the seas, arms limitations, self-determination, and more open economic relations. At home in America, Wilson's opponents made strong arguments that the peace treaty which the president negotiated was so different from his Fourteen Points that the treaty should be rejected.

Faced with this opposition, Wilson made one of the most important decisions of his political career. He decided to take his campaign to the people. He said that his opponents were isolationists who had poisoned public opinion. The president set out on an incredibly intensive speaking tour in September 1919. His doctor recommended that he not make the trip. Three weeks later President Wilson suffered a stroke in Colorado, and he was an invalid for the rest of his

***Figure 10** President Wilson, on the far right, pictured with the prime ministers of France, Italy, and Great Britain in Versailles, France, 1919. Wilson's visit was the first time a president had left the U.S. while in office.*

presidency. He could not continue to fight for his treaty, and he had not realized how tired the Americans were of war. The public seemed to want a return to happier times. In 1920 the Senate rejected Wilson's treaty by fourteen votes—the United States could not join the League of Nations. Later that year Warren G. Harding was elected president; he promised a "return to normalcy," and that apparently was what the American people wanted.

America was confused about what kind of foreign policy it should have. In the late nineteenth and early twentieth centuries the United States wanted to expand its economic, political, and moral influence. The country was successful in doing this, but the success created problems. As American influence grew, people in America and in other countries expected the United States to accept more responsibilities in the world. Americans were very reluctant to do this. After World War I the nation decided not to become a leader in world politics. Instead, America tried to return to the situation that existed from 1880–1914. During that time America did not have many outside responsibilities in the world, and the country could choose the spheres of influence where it would have the most effect.

After World War I the countries that won the war wanted to create an international system which would prevent any future major wars. They failed to build an effective international system because they never worked with one another. Britain and France followed very different lines of policy which often conflicted directly. The United States withdrew as much as possible from the world arena. President Wilson had recognized these problems. No one knows whether his foreign policy ideas would have done a better job of preventing World War II, but it is clear that the alternatives did not work.

American foreign policy went back into hibernation for the next twenty years, until the start of World War II. There was an attempt to turn the clock back on foreign policy not only beyond 1917 but even beyond 1898 and the Spanish-American War. Following World War I the United States was, without doubt, the most powerful nation in the world—economically, financially, politically, and militarily. American bankers and corporations were playing critical international roles, yet the U.S. Government returned to a more isolationist foreign policy. Tariffs are taxes on products coming from other countries. These taxes cause the prices for foreign goods to increase, thereby causing the demand to decrease. The government also demanded that America's wartime allies repay their war debts to the United States even though that created serious problems for the allies' economies. America also refused to join any international political organizations, including the World Court and the League of Nations.

Americans still talked about world peace, but they would not take any concrete steps to guarantee peace. In 1928 the United States sponsored the Kellogg-Briand Pact. In this agreement, over sixty nations renounced war and agreed to accept settlements of all disputes solely by peaceful means. That sounded good, but there was no way to make other countries rely only on peaceful means. The Pact had no strength behind it. The Pact made Americans feel good because the message to other countries was to "cast off evil." Unfortunately, nothing could be done once evil appeared, as it did in Germany under Adolf Hitler.

The high point of America's keeping its distance from the rest of the world occurred in the 1930s. Congress passed a series of neutrality laws, which meant that America could not take sides in any international arguments. Congress said that the U.S. government could not make loans or sales of arms to any nations at war. Only after Germany invaded Poland did Congress abolish this law.

***Figure 11** Uncle Sam sitting on a brittle perch, surrounded by Nazi bombs and clutching tightly to the policy of isolation. As the Nazis grew more powerful, isolationism became less popular in the U.S.*

Figure 12 Isolationist America watches from the other side of the Atlantic as Europe is consumed by the flames of war.

CONCLUSION

The sketch of American foreign policy from the 1780s through the 1920s and 1930s shows that the original ideas of the American political culture continued to have a strong effect on American foreign policy. The influence of the people is probably greater in the United States than in any other country. From the very start of American foreign policy under George Washington, the tradition was to remain separate from the problems of other countries. The first major theme of American foreign policy was isolationism.

Although the country was actively involved in world affairs in 1898 with the Spanish-American War in 1917 with World War I, America was quick to retreat from these roles. The U.S. actions in 1898 and 1917 seemed to be crusades to solve a problem. But these crusades were the exceptions to the idea that America's true purpose was to save the world by setting a good example at home rather than abroad.

This idea that the country should provide a model for the rest of the world was the second major theme of American foreign policy.

The relationship of these two themes—(1) isolationism and (2) America as a model for the world—was never completely clear. The development of the Monroe Doctrine reflects this. The doctrine announced to the world that the Western Hemisphere belonged to America's sphere of influence, and other countries should not make problems in this area. As the United States became more of a world power, however, there was more of a temptation to force other countries to accept the American model. America's definition of the Monroe Doctrine kept getting broader and broader throughout the nineteenth century.

Theodore Roosevelt and Woodrow Wilson were very aware of the Monroe Doctrine. Roosevelt understood it to say that the United States could be a policeman in its own hemisphere to settle problems between other countries. In the twenty five years after 1898, U.S. soldiers landed in Cuba, Puerto Rico, the Dominican Republic, Haiti, Nicaragua, Honduras, Panama, and Mexico. These countries were treated as *protectorates* of the United States and the American influence was great even after the troops departed. Wilson also felt that the country should be more active in international relations, and he insisted that the Monroe Doctrine be officially recognized in the League of Nations treaty.

The American people, however, were not ready to accept full responsibility in world politics. America was torn between wanting to project its power and influence to all corners of the globe and not wanting to be vulnerable to events in the rest of the world. American foreign policy was remarkably inconsistent in the period from 1898–1940. One reason for this inconsistency was that the goals of the policy kept shifting: America was not sure if it wanted to be a world leader. Another reason was that responsibility for foreign policy kept shifting between the president and the Congress. The Constitution made sure that power would be shared in the American system, and this had an effect on foreign policy, since both the president and the Congress wanted to control it.

American foreign policy was faced with goals that sometimes conflicted, institutions that competed with one another, and America's increasing importance in the world. Only after World War II did the American approach to foreign policy change dramatically because of these problems. The real revolution in American foreign policy occured after 1945, and we will examine the changes in the next chapter. America finally acknowledged its role in the world as a "superpower," but it will not be a surprise to find out that the old political ideas that influenced American policy for the first 165 years of the country's history remained important.

REVIEW QUESTIONS

1. Why do we say that the president's main power is the "power to persuade"?
2. What role can Congress perform best in foreign policy-making? What happens if Congress gets involved in the details of day-to-day foreign pol-

icy? Why did Congress pass the War Powers Act of 1973?

3. How do the president and Congress work together to make foreign policy?
4. How does the Constitution establish an open "invitation to struggle"?
5. What kind of connections with Europe did President George Washington recommend in his 1796 Farewell Address?
6. Describe the policy of the Monroe Doctrine. How did it change during the nineteenth century?
7. How did the American people respond to the Spanish-American War? What was America's goal in the war? What difficult choices did America face after the war?
8. Describe President Woodrow Wilson's League of Nations. What is the difference between a "balance of power" system and "collective security"?
9. Describe the mood of America about international affairs during the 1920's and 1930's.

3 Postwar Foreign Policy

Did Americans recognize the need for a completely new approach to foreign policy after World War II?
How has the critical importance of the Soviet-American relationship influenced American foreign policy?
What are the differences between the Cold War Era and the Detente Era in postwar foreign policy?
What impact did the Vietnam War have on U.S. foreign policy and America's position in the world?
How have views on detente changed in the last fifteen years?

American foreign policy after 1945 changed dramatically. To understand the new policy, we have to recognize what happened in American history before 1945. But that alone is not enough. The context for world politics after 1945 was almost entirely new. We can understand U.S. foreign policy only if we recognize the new factors. This chapter concentrates on three questions to help us understand foreign policy after 1945:

- *When World War II ended, how well did the United States recognize that American foreign policy would have to be completely different than it had been before the war?*
- *How has the United States responded to the new factors and conditions in world politics since the end of World War II?*
- *How has the Soviet-American relationship affected U.S. foreign policy?*

THE NEW WORLD OF FOREIGN POLICY AFTER 1945

Franklin Roosevelt died in April 1945, and Vice President Harry Truman succeeded him. One month later, in May 1945, the war in Europe came to an end. The war in the Pacific was over in August 1945. How was the new president supposed to provide leadership? A strong president like Woodrow Wilson had not been able to convince Americans and the world to accept his peace plans after World War I, and now America had an unknown and untested president.

Truman and the country did not have a vision of how to achieve peace, but the Western world watched anxiously. They realized that the failure to find a formula for peace after World War I led directly to another devastating war twenty years later and the deaths of over 50 million people. The Versailles Peace Treaty of 1919 did not work because it ignored the realities of world politics. The treaty split up the old Austrian-Hungarian Empire, but it left the new countries of Eastern Europe in a weak condition. It did not try to integrate Germany or the Soviet union into the international system. These unsolved issues were key causes of World War II.

At the end of World War I the leaders sat down

together, determined to reach a fair settlement so that there would be no more "great wars." They failed. At the end of World War II, in contrast, the victors started quarreling with one another immediately after the war, and no peace conference was ever held. The post-1945 settlement was not a triumph of fairness or justice. It divided nations like Germany, Austria, and Korea because the United States and the Soviet Union could not agree on whose soldiers should withdraw first. Countries in Eastern Europe lost their independence as they became part of the Soviet "sphere of influence."

The remarkable fact is that the arrangements made after World War II have worked. They have created stability in the West for over forty years. One historian suggests that in a hundred years people will call the period after World War II "the long peace."

One reason for this "extended" peace is that the international system is **bi-polar.** There is a division of many of the countries in the world into two poles, or parts. The United States and its allies are on one side, and the Soviet Union and its allies are on the other side. As a result, the central issue of American foreign policy for the last forty years has been the Soviet Union. America struggled, particularly in the first few years after 1945, to decide how to deal with the Soviet Union. The United States decided to try to limit Soviet influence through a policy of **containment**: America wanted to stop the Soviets from taking over other countries and expanding their influence. Today America is still not sure how to deal with the Soviet Union.

There were two kinds of revolutions in 1945. One was a political revolution with the world divided into

Figure 13 Winston Churchill of Great Britain, President Truman, and Josef Stalin of the Soviet Union at the Potsdam Conference in 1945. The disagreements between Stalin and Truman over withdrawal of troops from Europe after the war resulted in the Soviet occupation of Eastern Europe. Churchill warned of these problems in his famous "Iron Curtain" speech.

the American and the Soviet camps. The other revolution was technological: Nuclear weapons could be built. Nuclear weapons have made the world's most powerful nations much less willing to risk war with each other than they would have been in the past.

American and Soviet leaders have usually been cautious in dealing with each other. Several crises in Soviet-American relations might have produced a war if the leaders had not been so cautious.

- *In 1948 and 1961 the Soviets created conflicts in Berlin, the city which most reflects the bipolar division of the world. In 1948 the Soviets blocked all deliveries of food to West Berlin, but the Americans responded with a massive airlift which supplied the city for a year. In 1961 the Soviets split the city by constructing the Berlin Wall.*
- *In 1962 the Cuban Missile Crisis brought the world close to a nuclear war. The United States reacted strongly to the missiles which the Soviets were putting in Cuba, but America also left the Soviet Union with a chance to back down from its position without losing honor.*
- *In 1973 the United States supported Israel in the Yom Kippur War while the Soviet Union supported the forces attacking Israel.*
- *In 1979 the Soviets invaded Afghanistan. This particularly worried the United States because it brought the Soviets one step closer to the rich oil countries of the Persian Gulf.*
- *In 1983 the Soviets shot down a Korean passenger jumbo jet, killing everyone on board, including a U.S. Congressman. The United States saw this as an unnecesary direct challenge to the West.*

Fortunately, leaders on both sides have learned to keep cool heads even in dangerous crises.

It is probably fair to say that the stability and "long peace" after World War II have largely been a matter of luck. The luck is due partly to the division of the world into American and Soviet "spheres of influence" and partly to the effect of nuclear weapons. Until 1940, presidents saw one major task for American foreign policy: keep the country out of war. After 1945 the picture became more complicated.

America could no longer hide its head in the sand. Isolationism became almost impossible for the United States because of (a) the undeniable fact that America was now the world's most powerful country, (b) American hostility toward the Soviet Union, and (c) the obvious failure of America's policy of isolationism in the 1930s. After 1945, American presidents had two central foreign policy tasks: keep the peace, and stop Communism.

Americans recognized that the situation after 1945 was completely different than before the war. It called for a new foreign policy, but no one was quite sure what it should be. Probably no one visualized the global reach that America would develop or even the "entangling" military alliances that the United States would join. By the mid-1950s America had alliances with over forty countries, and by 1957 the American army had soldiers stationed in over fifty countries. Dean Acheson, the secretary of state under President Truman, described the enormous foreign policy challenge which America faced after the war. He said that the task was "just a little bit less formidable than that described in the first Chapter of Genesis. That was to create a world out of chaos: ours to create half a world, a free half, out of the same material without blowing the whole to pieces in the process."

The challenge was so great and America's role was so important that Congress reacted differently than after most wars. Wars magnify the power of the president, but Congress generally tries to regain its influence after the war. In domestic politics, Congress struck back at the president after the Civil War and after World War I. Congress also struck back after World War II by passing a Constitutional amendment limiting the president to two terms (Franklin Roosevelt had been elected four times). In foreign policy the Congress had also limited the president's power after a war. Congress rejected President Lincoln's plans for reconstruction after the Civil War and President Wilson's League of Nations after World War I. But Congress left President Truman with his foreign policy powers intact after 1945 because the situation was so complicated and dangerous.

In fact, America had to organize its government in a new way to deal with the country's new responsibilities. Until World War II the United States believed that foreign policy was something to be carried out in peacetime, and military policy was something to be followed in wartime. After the war, foreign and military policies had to be combined. The government had to grow to take care of its new worldwide responsibilities. The State Department was reorganized and enlarged. The old War and Navy Departments were combined into the Department of Defense. The National Security Council was created as a new and powerful force to cooordinate foreign policy for the president.

After World War II, the American people recognized that no "grand solution" like the League of Nations or the United Nations would put an end to war. Because of this, Americans were more willing to accept the struggle for power and the need to rely on military strength and a "balance of power."

The American policies in the first few years were bold and imaginative. They aimed at bringing about peace in the world, but the peace did not come, mainly due to the conflicting views of the world which the United States and the Soviet Union have. We now turn to the Soviet-American relationship because it shows best how American foreign policy changed in these years.

THE SOVIET-AMERICAN RELATIONSHIP

Through several centuries of history, the Soviet Union and the United States have never fought a war against each other, but American foreign policy after 1945 has concentrated on stopping the spread of Soviet influence. The American leaders have gone back and forth between completely distrusting the Soviets and trying to work with them to find peace. During the **Cold War** period from 1947 until the Cuban Missile Crisis in 1962, the danger of war between America and the Soviet Union was greatest, and the words used by both countries were angriest.

The Cuban Missile Crisis was a turning point toward less dangerous relations. It allowed a move to more discussions, arms control negotiations, and eventually a formal policy of **detente,** or a relaxation of tensions between the countries. By the end of the 1970s and in the early 1980s, however, the Soviet military build-up and Soviet actions in Afghanistan and Poland brought out all the old American suspicions. With President Reagan, there seemed to be a return to the Cold War. He condemned the Soviet Union as an "evil empire." The United States felt that it had to increase its military strength sharply to counter the Soviet military. Cooperation returned only when the new Soviet General Secretary Mikhail Gorbachev gave signs that the Soviets and Americans could work together again.

We can look at Soviet-U.S. relations in these three periods—the Cold War, the Cuban Missile Crisis, and the Reagan Administration—to get an understanding of how American foreign policy developed. In 1945 neither the Americans nor the Soviets expected American troops to stay in Europe. Ten months after the end of the war the number of U.S. soldiers in Europe dropped from over 3.5 million to four hundred thousand. By the 1950s, though, the Americans wanted their troops to stay, and an American general was commanding a Supreme Headquarters Allied Forces Europe. Those few years saw intense discussions about American foreign policy, and the decisions that were made then still shape present policy.

The U.S. soldiers remain in Europe today, well over forty years after the war. The question is often asked whether a different American foreign policy could have avoided the Soviet-American rivalry. The answer, as we shall see, is probably not.

THE COLD WAR ERA AND THE DOCTRINE OF "CONTAINMENT"

The term "Cold War" was first used in the late 1940s to describe the hostile relationship that had developed between the Soviet Union and the West. The conflict between the two sides was intense, but neither side seemed to want a war.

The United States and the Soviet Union had been allies during World War II (although they were each wary and cautious about the other). President Roosevelt wanted to cooperate with the Soviets after the war as well. He recognized that the interests of a huge country like the Soviet Union had to be considered in the international system, or another war could occur. President Truman shared Roosevelt's view, but Truman gradually concluded that U.S.-Soviet cooperation could not work. The Soviets were simply too suspicious of the United States and the rest of the world.

The Iron Curtain. Truman's acceptance of the Cold War was slow. Winston Churchill was much more convinced that the Soviets would not live up to their wartime promises to hold free elections in Eastern Europe and withdraw Soviet troops from the eastern part of Germany. Churchill pleaded with Truman to keep more American soldiers in Europe. In early 1946 Churchill went directly to the American people with his worries. In a famous speech given in Fulton, Missouri, Churchill said that the Soviet Union wanted to expand its power, and that "an iron curtain has descended across the continent." This was the first reference to the **Iron Curtain.** It marked the dividing line between the democratic countries of Western Europe and the Communist countries of Eastern Europe. Churchill was saying in blunt words that the Cold War had already begun. He wanted the British Commonwealth and the United States to oppose Soviet power.

At first, President Truman was reluctant to agree with Churchill. He and many Americans preferred to believe that the Soviets had limited goals and that the Soviet Union was just thinking about its own security needs. The picture soon started to change when it looked as if the Soviets were putting pressure on the governments of Turkey, Iran, and Greece. By 1948 the Western nations were even more worried about Soviet actions in Czechoslovakia and Berlin.

The Principle of Containment. George F. Kennan, the leading American expert on the Soviet Union, developed the idea that the Soviets were ready to test any "soft spot" in neighboring countries to see if they could expand their influence. According to Kennan, the challenge for the West was to make the risks too great for the Soviets to attack the soft spots. This was the doctrine of *containment*—Western firmness would limit the Soviet expansion of influence. Soviet policy was seen as always pushing and looking for weak spots. Kennan's recommendation was for an American foreign policy of "long-term, patient but firm and vigilant containment."

Kennan claimed that the Soviet thinking about how to make government policy is very different from American thinking. This is due to the way that Russian history, national character, and Communist ideology (the set of ideas about Communism that the Soviets believe) interact. In this view the Soviets would not cooperate with non-Communist countries, and they would use pressure constantly to reach their goals. Kennan wanted American foreign policy to stop the Soviet pressure, but he did not want to use the American military to do this. Instead, Kennan wanted to rely on American economic aid to build up the economies in Western Europe and Japan. If the national economies were strong, the countries would have the self-confidence to resist the Soviets on their own.

The Truman Doctrine. The emphasis on economics is a key point. The goal of the United States was not to defeat the Soviet Union militarily or destroy the Soviet state. The goal was to limit the influence of the Soviet Union by providing economic aid to other countries. President Truman made this clear in the **Truman Doctrine,** announced in a March 1947 speech.

The Truman Doctrine

. . . totalitarian regimes imposed on free peoples, by direct or indirect aggression, undermine the foundations of internal peace and hence the security of the United States.

The peoples of a number of countries of the world have recently had totalitarian regimes forced upon them against their will. . . . I believe that we must assist free peoples to work out their own destinies in their own way. I believe that our help should be primarily through economic and financial aid which is essential to economic stability and orderly political processes. . . .

The seeds of totalitarian regimes . . . reach their full growth when the hope of a people for a better life has died. We must keep that hope alive. The free peoples of the world look to us for support in maintaining their freedoms. If we falter in our leadership, we may endanger the peace of the world—and we shall surely endanger the welfare of our own nation.

Truman's speech was as important as George Washington's Farewell Address or James Monroe's speech announcing the Monroe Doctrine. Truman announced a completely new foreign policy. Henry Kissinger says that the burst of creativity in foreign policy that started with the Truman Doctrine was "one of the glorious moments of American history." Americans had to act fast in 1947. They suddenly saw how all the other countries who fought World War II were suffering. Some countries were on the brink of collapsing.

Britain informed the United States in February 1947 that it could no longer protect Greece and Turkey from Soviet pressure. Throughout the nineteenth century and the first part of the twentieth century, America had depended on Britain to maintain the balance of power which protected the United States. Now, all of a sudden, no one could protect the United States except the country itself.

The Success of Truman's Foreign Policy. Truman acted quickly and firmly. He directed American foreign policy along a path that basically is still followed. Truman's policies were a creative triumph. The steps which Truman took included:

- *defending the Eastern Mediterranean countries like Greece and Turkey from the Soviet Union;*
- *rebuilding the broken-down economies of Europe through the Marshall Plan;*
- *forming a military alliance, the North Atlantic Treaty Organization (NATO), to defend the West;*

- *starting programs to make Germany and Japan, our former enemies, into democracies;*
- *providing military aid to friendly countries under attack.*

No great power in history has ever been as generous in helping other countries, including former enemies, as America was after 1945. Of course there were benefits for the United States and the goal of containing the Soviets was obvious, but the country was very willing to support non-American centers of strength in Europe with American money.

The Marshall Plan and the Formation of NATO. America was the doctor and Europe was the sick patient—and the prescription for a cure was a huge injection of American money. This took place through the **Marshall Plan,** announced in June 1947. The Marshall Plan showed the incredible American willingness to sacrifice in order to build up Europe. The United States did not loan the money to the European countries for recovery. It gave them the money, and America demanded only that the European states cooperate with one another economically.

Over the four-year period of the Marshall Plan, Congress agreed to give $13.3 billion for European recovery. This was an incredible amount of money at the time, and it was critical for saving Europe from disaster. Secretary of State George Shultz described in 1987 how unique the Marshall Plan was because it managed to benefit both the United States and Europe. In his words:

> The success of the Marshall Plan 40 years ago demonstrates that foreign affairs is not always a "zero-sum game." We do not necessarily advance our own

vital interests at another nation's cost. On the contrary, more often than not, the most effective way of promoting our basic goals is by working with others to achieve their basic goals. That is what a Democratic President and a Republican Congress understood in 1947 when they allocated 11 cents out of every Federal dollar to fund the Marshall Plan.

In fact, the U.S. aid was offered to the Soviet Union and Eastern Europe too, but it was refused. The Soviets were afraid to let the American "capitalists" have any influence on their economy, and they did not want a stable Europe. The Soviets preferred insta-

***Figure 14** A brand-new Mack truck arrives in Le Havre to help with the rebuilding of war-ravaged France, courtesy of the Marshall Plan, 1948.*

bility because there would be a better chance for a revolution in their favor.

The Marshall Plan was not enough, by itself, to make the Europeans feel comfortable. In 1948 the Soviets overran Czechoslovakia and put a blockade around West Berlin. People in Europe started comparing the Soviet leader Joseph Stalin to Adolf Hitler. American foreign policy also had to provide military security for Europe because the European people could not work hard for economic recovery if they thought they would be conquered the next day.

Some European states began talking about alliances to protect themselves from the Soviets in 1947 and 1948. In April 1949 the United States agreed with eleven other countries to provide mutual military support through the North Atlantic Treaty. The U.S. Senate accepted the treaty that summer, and NATO became the heart of American defense policy—and it remains so today. The American decision to join NATO was remarkable because it was the first time ever that the United States joined an alliance in peacetime. Europe became America's "first line of defense." The success of NATO has also been remarkable. There are debates and disagreements among the members of NATO, but the alliance has held together and is still keeping the peace.

The Problems with Containment. The central foreign policy idea in these years was containment. By 1949 it was recognized officially as American policy in a famous National Security Council paper reviewing American foreign policy. Containment aimed to change Soviet behavior by offering a combination of "sticks" and "carrots." The sticks were to punish the

Figure 15 NATO soldiers on maneuvers in Germany, 1982. The NATO alliance has helped to ensure the security of Western Europe from 1949 to the present day.

Soviets if they did not change their actions; the carrots were to reward them if they did. George Kennan, the father of the containment idea, complained that America forgot the carrots. The Soviets did make some changes, but America never rewarded the Soviets for them.

Containment created two kinds of problems for the United States. First, people had different understandings and definitions of containment. Originally, containment was supposed to be used only for certain important "soft spots." Some American leaders, however, started thinking that containment meant acting against the Soviets wherever there was trouble. The Americans were quick to blame the Soviets for all problems—for example, in Vietnam—when sometimes the problems had other causes. Second, containment created problems because the Americans never made it clear exactly what behavior they expected from the Soviets. The message to the Soviets was unclear.

In general, a different American foreign policy would not have mattered. The world was bipolar after World War II, and the Soviet Union did not want to accept any arrangement giving the United States more influence. One expert on the Soviets said that the United States could have given the Soviet Union the atomic bomb and an economic aid package, and the Soviets would still have been suspicious. The Soviet Union was especially worried because America had the atomic bomb. American and Soviet interests were so different that competition and conflict was probably unavoidable. Both the Soviet Union and the United States wanted to expand their interests, but they did it in different ways. The Soviet expansion of interests took place *against* the wishes of other countries. The American expansion of interests, on the other hand, took place at the invitation of other countries who were worried about the Soviet Union.

THE CUBAN MISSILE CRISIS AS A TURNING POINT IN U.S. FOREIGN POLICY

The Cold War continued in the 1950s. There were hopes that it would let up because President Dwight D. Eisenhower and Soviet General Secretary Nikita Khrushchev seemed to be able to talk to each other. By the mid-1950s both sides had huge numbers of deadly nuclear weapons. It appeared that Eisenhower and Khrushchev both wanted to slow down the race to build more weapons. Then, however, Khrushchev started a series of actions in 1958 that led to the 1962 Cuban Missile Crisis. Khrushchev started the discussion about how to divide Germany between the East and the West again. He wanted NATO out of West Berlin, and he eventually let the Berlin Wall be built in 1961 to stop the flood of East Germans escaping to West Germany. The Soviets also exaggerated their missile build-up to impress and worry the West.

When Americans and the Kennedy Administration learned in October 1962 that the Soviets had built launch sites for about seventy missiles in Cuba, ninety miles from the United States, they felt that they had to react strongly. American reports showed that the new Soviet missiles were directed at American cities. The nuclear warheads amounted to half the nuclear-warhead potential in the entire Soviet Union. Khrushchev seemed to be daring the United States to do something. He had seen President Kennedy hesitate—first, to overthrow the Cuban leader Fidel Castro in 1961, and second, to prevent the building of the Berlin Wall.

Khrushchev also felt that the Soviets were in a weak position militarily. The West had discovered that the Soviet missiles were not as advanced as Khrushchev had been saying. If the Soviets could install missiles in Cuba, Khrushchev's missile problem would be solved while making the Americans look weak. Khrushchev wanted to make the Europeans think that the Americans did not have the courage to stand up to the Soviets.

The Crisis: Britain's Harold Macmillan called the Cuban Missile Crisis "one of the great turning points

Figure 16 President Kennedy and Soviet General Secretary Nikita Khrushchev in Vienna, 1961. The two men would communicate again under less friendly terms in October of 1962, during the Cuban Missile Crisis.

in history." Others called it "the Gettysburg of the Cold War." Robert Kennedy referred to it simply as "The Thirteen Days," implying what a dangerous crisis it was.

In September 1962 President Kennedy was informed that Soviet military parts were being delivered to Cuba, but he was assured that they were not

Figure 17 Cuban President Fidel Castro pictured with a Soviet missile in place of his trademark cigar. With Soviet missiles, Castro's Cuba would be a threat to U.S. security.

dangerous. Only in mid-October did the president learn that the Soviets would have 16–24 nuclear missiles ready to fire in two weeks. He quickly called emergency meetings of his top advisers. Talks with the Soviets were not helpful, so President Kennedy went on national television on October 22 to explain the emergency.

Kennedy's advisers debated whether to launch an invasion, bomb the missile sites, or establish a naval blockade to stop any more Soviet deliveries. They finally chose a naval blockade, or "quarantine" as they called it. One message from the Soviets indicated a willingness to cooperate, but a later message was more "hard-line." President Kennedy ignored the second message and indicated that he would accept the first message. The United States promised not to invade Cuba if the Soviet missiles would be removed. This was an offer that did not embarrass the Soviets. On October 28 the Soviets accepted those terms. The crisis was over.

The Effects of the Crisis. In this case, Khrushchev

had acted too quickly. He had pressured the United States too close to home—he had forgotten the Monroe Doctrine! The Americans would not let the Soviet leader get away with his dare. As Americans saw the continuing crisis in Berlin and the Cuban Missile Crisis, they realized that they had to think again about keeping a "frontier," or a border, around the Communist world. The old ideas on containment needed some rethinking.

The results of the Cuban Missile Crisis are very important. The crisis was a historical turning point because it marked the end of the Cold War and the beginning of American and Soviet efforts to discover a more peaceful way to act toward each other. The United States stood up to the Soviets and forced them to pull back their missiles and remove their launchers. But the Cuban Missile Crisis should not just be seen as an American victory. President Kennedy took great care not to embarrass the Soviets. Kennedy let the Soviets "save face." The foreign policy lesson for the United States was to move away from the Cold War. After 1962 the Americans tried to rely more on arms control and detente for Soviet-American relations. The Soviets and Americans were both scared by how close they had come to a nuclear war, and they worked hard to reduce the future chances for war.

The tensions between the Soviet Union and the United States relaxed after the Cuban Missile Crisis. Khrushchev stopped acting aggressively. Kennedy was seen in the West as a hero because of his firm but flexible and rational actions. Since the president had proved his strength and competence, he could now negotiate with the Soviets and make concessions without people saying that he was "soft" on communism. In 1963 Kennedy and Khrushchev signed a significant treaty banning all above-ground nuclear tests. They also agreed to install a "hot line" so they could talk with each other in a crisis.

The Cuban Missile Crisis signaled a shift in U.S.-Soviet relations from the Cold War to a period of working together more closely. It was the start of the era of detente, but the seeds of new problems were also visible. Another lesson for the Soviets from the Cuban Missile Crisis, for example, was never to let the Americans make the Soviet Union back down again. The Soviets, therefore, began a long-term program of building up all categories of their military power—missiles, bombers, tanks, submarines, and fighter planes. Likewise, the Soviets had a different understanding of the meaning of detente. The Americans felt that detente would lead to genuine friendship and the ability to work together. The Soviets saw detente only as a means of allowing the two countries to coexist and tolerate each other. The Soviets had fewer expectations from detente than the Americans.

Nonetheless, the key message from the Cuban Missile Crisis for American foreign policy was the new picture of the Soviet Union. The country was not seen as a total enemy, just as another opponent with limited resources. President Kennedy urged Americans to reconsider their views on the Cold War. He told people not to take "a distorted and desparate view of the other side, not to see conflicts as inevitable." He also said that "no government or social system is so evil that its people must be considered as lacking in virtue." Containment had been based on the "devil image" of the Soviet Union. It no longer seemed appropriate. The harsh views of the Cold War seemed less necessary.

THE EFFECT OF THE VIETNAM WAR ON U.S. FOREIGN POLICY

Foreign policy is always changing. The shock of the Cuban Missile Crisis helped Americans realize that it was time to move away from the ideas of the Cold War. Likewise, the tragic war in Vietnam forced Americans to see the shortcoming of containment in U.S. foreign policy. Containment policy with its bipolar view of the world led Americans to see the Vietnam War as part of Soviet-American hostilities. The United States assumed that a solution could be found either through a policy of strength with the Soviets or a policy of detente. In fact, neither policy worked. The roots of the war went deep into Vietnam's history. Through the futile war, the United States discovered that its power was limited against such domestic factors.

The whole basis of American foreign policy was shaken by the Vitenam War. Questions had to be asked about the basic ideas behind the policy: (1) How wise was the American policy of being ready to fight "limited wars" throughout the world in order to protect small democratic countries? and (2) Was the containment idea still appropriate after the Cold War period? The American view of the world tended to see the "free world" versus the Communists in a battle to win the hearts and minds of the rest of the world. Many Americans felt that the country had stopped the spread of Communism by fighting a conventional war in Korea and by staring down the

Soviets in the Cuban Missile Crisis. Stopping the Communists in a guerrilla war would complete the picture and teach the Communists a lesson. (In *guerrilla wars,* armies do not have regular soldiers but instead depend on volunteers who join together for attacks but then disappear back into the jungle or the villages. Fighting against a guerrilla army is frustrating because it is hard to identify the enemy.) America wanted to save South Vietnam, but it was never clearly defined how the United States would do that or how success would be measured.

Background. The war in Vietnam was the longest

Figure 18 The guerrilla war in Vietnam was difficult and frustrating for American soldiers, who fought an elusive enemy in rugged terrain.

and most frustrating war that the United States has ever fought. It was a nightmare for America to lose a major war, suffer over fifty thousand deaths, send over five hundred thousand soldiers to fight in Vietnam, and alienate thousands of other Americans, many of them young, who protested against the war. The divisions within the country were so deep that President Lyndon Johnson decided not to run for reelection as president because his policies were so unpopular.

America's war in Vietnam started in the mid-1960s, but the battle really started in 1950, or perhaps in 1930 when the Indochinese Communist Party was founded. (Vietnam used to be called *Indochina.)* From then until the collapse of South Vietnam in 1975, the Party never changed its goal of a unified, Communist Vietnam. The Vietnamese Communists had to fight against the Japanese in the 1940s, the French in the 1950s, and the Americans in the 1960s and 1970s. They saw the fight as a struggle for the goal of unification, not as a fight against any country.

From 1950–65 the U.S. foreign policy toward Vietnam was an economic aid program. The United States wanted to contain the Communist threat in Asia, as well as in Europe. The French withdrew from Indochina in 1954, and the United States quickly moved in to aid the new nation of South Vietnam in maintaining its pro-Western independence. Only Korea received more American economic and military aid in the 1955–61 period. By 1963 South Vietnam received more American military aid than any other country.

The American Response. In 1965 it looked as if the

violence in Vietnam might lead to the fall of the South Vietnamese government. President Johnson made a major change in U.S. foreign policy by sending thousands of American troops to Vietnam. Even in 1967 the U.S. military leaders were confident that they would win the war, but the number of Americans who felt that the United States had made a mistake sending troops to fight in Vietnam was growing:

	Percent of Americans disagreeing with Vietnam War
August, 1965	24
March, 1966	25
November, 1966	31
February, 1967	32
July, 1967	42
October, 1967	46

The Communists launched a major attack called the Tet Offensive in early 1968, and this was so costly in terms of lives lost that the domestic debate in America became very serious. *Time* magazine asked whether "victory in Vietnam—or even a favorable settlement—may simply be beyond the grasp of the world's greatest power." More and more Americans spoke of withdrawal, or at least of a halt to the bombing.

One American journalist summed up the war very well. He said that the United States was a great but divided nation fighting a limited war; North Vietnam was a small but united nation waging total war. The North Vietnamese Communists had more "staying power" than the American leaders expected. The North Vietnamese suffered from the American attacks, but they were willing to accept these losses.

Figure 19 ***Anti-Vietnam War demonstrators outside of the Pentagon, October 1967.***

They felt that if they were patient, the Americans would grow tired of the war. The North Vietnamese were right.

Postwar American foreign policy had been basically bipartisan—in other words, the Democrats and Republicans generally agreed what to do. The Vietnam War broke up this bipartisanship. It also changed how Americans looked at foreign policy decision-making. Many people blamed the system of foreign policy-making for getting the country involved in the Vietnam War. They were hesitant to leave future decisions to the same people who had made policy in the past. The United States has never fully recovered from these problems. Even in the late 1980s, the country is still searching for a bipartisan foreign policy, and the issue of who makes foreign policy has never been fully resolved.

The Nixon-Kissinger Approach. Richard Nixon had pledged to end direct American involvement in the Vietnam War while he was campaigning to be president in 1968, but he gave no details on how to do this. Vietnam had a different significance for Nixon than it had for Johnson. Johnson committed the country to a massive involvement in Vietnam because he wanted to stop the spread of Communism. He seemed to believe in a **domino theory,** which meant that if one country fell to the Communists, then several others would fall, like dominoes. When Nixon became president, Communism did not appear so threatening. The Soviet and Chinese Communists were quarreling with each other, and the United States was exploring a friendlier relationship with

China. Detente with the Soviets also made the threat of Communism look less dangerous.

Nixon, with the help of his foreign policy adviser Henry Kissinger, developed a more realistic view of what America could do in the world. In what came to be called the "Nixon Doctrine," Nixon said that "America cannot—and will not—conceive *all* the decisions, and undertake *all* the defense of the free nations of the world. We will help where it makes a real difference and is considered in our interest."

Nixon's approach to getting the United States out of Vietnam was complicated. There was something to keep everyone happy. The plan included:

***Figure 20** President Nixon and Chairman Mao of China in Peking in 1972 after relations had been opened between the two countries.*

- *a Vietnamization program to reduce the number of American troops in Vietnam; this was designed to please the left-wing critics of the war;*
- *the goal of "peace with honor" to keep up American prestige and protect the South Vietnamese allies; this goal was primarily for the right-wing supporters of the war;*
- *secret negotiations with the North Vietnamese;*
- *increased bombing in North Vietnam, Cambodia, and Laos to put more pressure on the North Vietnamese to reach a settlement;*
- *discussions with the Soviets to have them help bring about a settlement.*

This strategy sounds comprehensive, but it was too complicated and full of contradictions. The "Vietnamization" process was supposed to quiet the protesters, but the increased bombing had the opposite effect. More and more Congressmen opposed the war, the U.S. allies in Europe increased their criticisms, and inflation due to the war grew worse.

Nixon wanted to end American involvement in 1968, but a final agreement was not reached until January 1973. That agreement only ended American involvement—not the war itself. The North Vietnamese were finally ready to bargain in 1972 because (1) their attack that year showed that the South Vietnamese forces were stronger than expected and (2) they feared that Nixon, once reelected, would be less willing to negotiate.

The agreement signed in January 1973 was by no means a solution to the problem. It was unworkable and vague. The North Vietnamese achieved what they wanted: a complete U.S. withdrawal. Two years later they launched a huge attack on South Vietnam and finally achieved the goal of a unified, Communist Vietnam. America was weary of the war, and Richard Nixon was gone as president because of the Watergate scandal. His successor, Gerald Ford, asked for $1.4 billion in military aid for Vietnam and Cambodia in early 1975, but Congress only agreed to $700 million. Americans wanted to put the war behind them.

Conclusion. The Vietnam War did not change the entire direction of American foreign policy, but it made clear that there were severe limitations to what the United States could do in the world. Containment was still the major idea of American foreign policy even after Vietnam, but it was viewed more cautiously. As Republican Senator William Cohen of Maine said, "The legacy of Vietnam does not mean that we will not send our sons anywhere. It does mean that we will not send them everywhere." One poll of Americans after Vietnam showed that the only country that the American people were still willing to defend from attack was Canada. The American people said "no more Vietnams."

The real problem was that America suffered a terrible identity crisis and period of self-doubt after Vietnam. Some people even favored a return to American isolationism, but most realized that this was impossible. The challenge after 1975 was to rediscover a purpose in American foreign policy.

DETENTE FROM NIXON TO REAGAN

The Detente Era. The period of detente lasted from the mid-1960s until the late 1970s, when the American people started to question its success. They were frustrated with America's defeat in Vietnam, with the taking of American hostages in Iran, and with the control of oil prices by the Middle Eastern countries. Americans wanted to know why U.S. power could not affect these developments.

Ronald Reagan expressed the frustration and impatience of many Americans very effectively in his campaigns to be president in 1976 and 1980. Reagan declared that the United States should take charge of its own foreign policy again. After the U.S. withdrawal from Vietnam, American foreign policy was very hesitant. No one wanted too much U.S. involvement in other trouble spots in the world. By 1980, however, American voters showed that they were ready to throw away the ghost of Vietnam and accept a new American "assertiveness" (a willingness to stand up confidently for U.S. policies). Reagan was elected in a sweeping victory.

The Reagan Administration came into power in 1981, promising a fundamental change in foreign policy, especially toward the Soviet Union. The president favored a new emphasis on America's importance in the world; he was against the old detente policies. The five presidents before Reagan had believed in detente in one way or another. The foreign policy of President Nixon and his advisor, Henry Kissinger, marked the high point for detente. Nixon and Kissinger really stretched the definition of the word well beyond the original meaning of "relaxation of tensions."

Detente Policy of Nixon and Kissinger. The Nixon and Kissinger strategy looked for a new kind of positive working relationship with the Soviet Union. First, the United States acknowledged finally that the Soviet Union should also be considered a superpower. Second, the strategy accepted the division of Eastern and Western Europe. West Germany started a policy of closer relations with the states of Eastern Europe in the late 1960s, and the Helsinki Agreement was signed in 1975. This agreement, signed by thirty five countries, was almost a post-World War II peace treaty. The Soviets and the East agreed to the treaty because it accepted as final the national borders of the postwar period. The United States and the West, on the other hand, signed the treaty because it guaranteed more emphasis on human rights and the free movement of people between countries.

The Nixon-Kissinger strategy also recommended more agreements with the Soviet Union. America agreed to increase economic and technical assistance to the Soviets. The hope was that better economic relations would "spillover" to improve U.S.-Soviet political relations. Over half the treaties or agreements that the United States had made with the Soviets from 1933 to 1980 were completed between 1969 and 1974. Nixon and Kissinger wanted to set up new rules of competition for the superpowers. They especially wanted to work out arms control agreements to reduce the dangers of a nuclear war.

The Problems with Detente Policy. The detente policy of Nixon and Kissinger started to fall apart in 1973. In the October 1973 Arab-Israeli war the Soviet Union did not try to stop its allies, Egypt and Syria, from attacking Israel. The Americans protested when the Soviets provided military supplies to the Arabs.

The Soviets' understanding of detente was also a problem. The Soviets felt that they could still support revolutions in other countries. The Soviets, for example, helped pay for Cuban soldiers to fight in Angola (in the southern part of Africa) in 1975. Americans felt that this did not fit in with a policy of detente.

Detente policy was more difficult for the American people to understand than the Cold War policy. It required a more complicated picture of the Soviet Union because the Soviets were supposed to be seen as somewhere between friends and enemies. Ronald Reagan challenged President Gerald Ford for the Republican presidential nomination in 1976 by attacking the detente policy which Ford tried to continue after Nixon resigned as president.

Ford's response to Reagan was to drop the word "detente" from his vocabulary and instead call his policy "Peace through Strength." Many Americans worried that the Soviet Union had taken advantage of detente to build up its own military strength. The Soviets seemed to be getting specific benefits such as American grain or technology, while the Americans only got promises of good behavior from the Soviets.

Once again, the question of Soviet intentions was at the center of American foreign policy. Ronald Reagan made it an issue in the 1976 presidential election, and he brought it up again in 1980 when he won the election. As of 1976, the mood in America had shifted. The people wanted their leaders to drive harder bargains with the Soviets. President Jimmy Carter's response was to give lower priority to relations with the Soviet Union. He paid more attention to other countries and to establishing a "world order." Carter tried to redesign detente on a more realistic basis, but the Soviets were not very cooperative because of Carter's "human rights" campaign. President Carter insisted that the United States could only have good relations with countries that respected the human rights of their citizens. The Soviets, however, saw the human rights campaign as an attack on their system.

The Reagan Alternative to Detente. The Reagan Administration blamed Carter's policy for underestimating the strength of the Soviet Union and letting American economic and military strength slip. (In fact, Reagan's criticisms were also aimed at President Ford and Nixon, but because they were fellow Republicans Reagan did not mention them.) Reagan promised to follow a more aggressive and confrontational foreign policy. He hoped that the Soviets would observe America's strong policy and therefore change their policy to be more positive. The Americans would try to force the Soviets to change their behavior by building up a position of strength.

This was not a new idea. It was exactly what containment was supposed to do. Containment, though, was originally supposed to rely on economic strength—hence, the Marshall Plan. The Reagan foreign policy, in contrast, relied on huge build-up of military strength. In some ways, Ronald Reagan gave up on detente and returned to the foreign policy of the 1940s and 1950s, but with a new twist—military strength.

Containment had been thought of as a defensive strategy to stop Russian influence. The Reagan strategy was an offensive approach. The military strategy

Figure 21 President Ronald Reagan speaking at Andrews Air Force Base in Maryland, 1985.

called for by President Reagan requires the United States to be able to fight several kinds of wars at the same time (for example, non-nuclear wars against enemies anywhere in the world, a non-nuclear war against the Soviet Union, or a nuclear war against the Soviets). To be able to fight all these wars is enormously expensive, so Reagan had to increase the defense budget sharply. Adding these new capabilities also increases the chances of a major war breaking out. The problem with Reagan's view of containment was that is was too expensive, too complicated to manage, and too dangerous.

The Reagan views softened a little after two or three years. This is typical for a new president. A new president usually begins his term by stressing his differences from the former president, but then he gradually makes compromises. With Reagan's Soviet policy, costs were one explanation for the changes. Pressures from Congress and from America's allies were a second explanation. Reagan's belief, though, that the Soviets were evil and the cause of most problems in the world did not change. Reagan blamed the Soviets for unrest whether it was in Central America or the Middle East, and he announced that America would help support anti-Soviet forces in those countries where Soviet-backed takeovers occur. This is the *Reagan Doctrine*. One example is the support given to the "Contras" in Nicaragua, who are fighting the Soviet-supported government.

The Influence of the Soviets. It is a mistake to think that U.S. foreign policy is only influenced by American factors. Changes in the Soviet Union have also had a major effect on U.S. policy. The Soviets have had four leaders in the 1980s. Those changes have caused some confusion. The present leader, Mikhail Gorbachev, has also given clear indications since becoming General Secretary of the Communist Party in March 1985 that he expects a new kind of foreign policy. He has said that "the current stage in the development of civilization . . . is dictating the need for an urgent, radical break with the traditions of political thinking." The Gorbachev foreign policy team has introduced several new initiatives ranging from arms control measures to efforts to reestablish ties with China.

Gorbachev, like Reagan, still sees a basically bipolar world. Gorbachev wants to carry out changes inside the Soviet Union, but he knows that he needs international stability to do that. Gorbachev, therefore, watches the United States carefully. Most of his foreign policy advisers are experts on the United States and its policies.

CONCLUSION

The greatest accomplishment of President Reagan's foreign policy has been the restoration of America's self-confidence. He used a military build-up and an assertive foreign policy to reestablish America's power in the world and to make Americans proud. The danger is that a war may be more likely with such aggressive steps. The Soviets have shown more willingness to negotiate with the United States recently. Whether this is due to Reagan's policy or to other factors inside Soviet politics is difficult to determine. In any case, it is clear that President Reagan's policies were not new but rather represented a return to some earlier postwar American foreign policy thinking.

REVIEW QUESTIONS

1. Describe America's new world role after 1945.
2. Why were the Truman Doctrine and the Marshall Plan significant? Why do people call these policies creative?
3. What was the containment policy? How was it linked to the Cold War and its bipolar views of the world?
4. What was America's thinking about military alliances before and after World War II? What is the significance of NATO?
5. What was the significance of the Cuban Missile Crisis for American foreign policy?
6. How did the Vietnam War show the limits of America's power?
7. How did the American public view the Vietnam War? Did this have an effect on U.S. policy?
8. What effect did the Vietnam War have on the foreign policy consensus within the country?
9. Describe the changing views of detente in the 1970s and 1980s. What was the attitude of Nixon and Kissinger toward detente? What was Reagan's attitude?
10. What has happened to Soviet-American relations during Ronald Reagan's administration?

4 The Changing Realities of American Foreign Policy

Will American foreign policy change significantly in the future?
Will the United States learn to cope with an interdependent world and "manage" rather than try to "solve" foreign policy problems?
Is America losing interest in international cooperation?
How can "realism" and "vision" be combined in American foreign policy?

We have looked at American foreign policy over a period of two hundred years. The message seems clear that the historical forces and traditions that influenced foreign policy in George Washington's time still have an effect today, but the dramatic changes in the world after 1945 forced America to take a more active role in international relations. Until 1945 the United States usually tried not to have a foreign policy, and Americans are often tempted even today to withdraw from the rest of the world. The question for us in this chapter, however, is how likely is it that American foreign policy will change significantly in the future? If we look ahead twenty to fifty years, will America lose its position as the most powerful country in the world? Will the world look hostile to the United States? Is bipolarity disappearing?

How well prepared is America to make foreign policy? In the 1830s a French observer of the United States wrote a classic book, *Democracy in America,* which is still widely read. The author, Alexis de Tocqueville, showed a deep understanding of developments in America. His points on foreign policy are often discussed, because he doubted that a democratic country could make good foreign policy. He wrote the following:

> I do not hesitate to say that it is especially in the conduct of foreign relations that democracies appear to me decidedly inferior to other governments. . . . Foreign politics demand scarcely any of those qualities which are peculiar to a democracy. . . . A democracy can only with great difficulty regulate the details of an important undertaking, persevere in a fixed design, and work out its execution in spite of serious obstacles. It cannot combine its measures with secrecy or await their consequences with patience.

These words continue to be amazingly appropriate for American foreign policy today. The United States still has problems sticking with one foreign policy concept. We tend to shift ideas every four years to correspond with our elections. Foreign policy is also very "public" in America, and people grow impatient rapidly if U.S. foreign policy does not work the way they want it to work. The American people are suspicious of negotiations that take too long, and the people have had doubts about secrecy ever since President Wilson's secret negotiations for the Treaty of Versailles in 1919.

In fact, even though presidents end up spending most of their time on foreign policy, they do not always have much experience prior to taking office. In the twentieth century before the 1988 election, thirty one people had been nominated to be president by major parties or had moved from vice president to president because of the president's death or resignation. Only ten of those thirty one had had real foreign policy experience. For example, both Theodore Roosevelt and Franklin Roosevelt had been assistant secretary of the navy. Herbert Hoover had played a key role in international economic policy. Richard Nixon, Lyndon Johnson, Hubert Humphrey, and Walter Mondale all had some foreign policy experience because they had been vice presidents. Most other nominees had no experience (for example, Calvin Coolidge, Jimmy Carter, and Ronald Reagan) or limited foreign policy experience as members of Congress (Harry Truman, John Kennedy, Gerald Ford).

Comparing periods of American foreign policy. Despite these problems with foreign policy, the United States has provided world leadership throughout the twentieth century, sometimes willingly and sometimes unwillingly. We can compare American foreign policy over several time periods, as described in Chapters 2 and 3. These comparisons can be made in terms of whether (a) the purpose of foreign policy was clear, (b) the U.S. leaders recognized what their goals were and what their chances were of reaching them, and (c) there was cooperation with other countries.

1. Early American foreign policy from George Washington through the nineteenth century had a clear purpose. It was to stay out of any political involvement with Europe, although commercial relations were possible. The United States had little military power to support the policies of the Monroe Doctrine, but the British navy provided the necessary protection. America did not cooperate with other countries at all.

2. U.S. foreign policy became much more active in the early twentieth century (1898–1920). This was the period that included the presidencies of Theodore Roosevelt and Woodrow Wilson. The purpose of foreign policy was vague. The country swung between wanting to use its power in the world to actively affect international developments (especially in Latin America) and wanting to serve as a passive model democracy for other countries. America used its strength to achieve its goals rather effectively, especially in World War I. International cooperation, however, was still limited. Americans continued to be reluctant to accept major responsibility.

3. During the Truman and Eisenhower administrations (1945–60) the purpose of American foreign policy—to contain the Soviet Union—was unmistakably clear. The Truman Doctrine, the Marshall

Plan, and the formation of NATO were imaginative and bold steps to deal with the new bipolar world. The United States relied on its economic superiority to reach its foreign policy goals. Most striking, America developed a completely new attitude toward cooperation. The country had never agreed to join any alliance in peacetime, but it joined several alliances beginning with NATO in 1949. U.S. foreign policy has never been as generous as during this period.

4. The Kennedy, Johnson, and Nixon administrations (1960–74) had to cope with the problem of American involvement in Vietnam. American foreign policy was sent into total confusion. In the early 1960s, foreign policy shifted from the Cold War period to a detente period. Discussions were not about the purpose of foreign policy but about the most effective strategy to use against the Russians. As the war in Vietnam increased in importance, however, the purpose of U.S. foreign policy became much harder to recognize. America discovered the limits of its power: military strength alone could not bring peace to Vietnam. People in the United States once again questioned the country's role in world politics. The consensus on American foreign policy fell apart.

5. The Carter and Reagan administration have had very different approaches to foreign policy. Carter's approach resembled Woodrow Wilson's policy: it had a moralistic tone. Reagan's approach relied more on American military strength to force others to accept U.S. foreign policy. To the rest of the world, the purpose of American foreign policy

in this period was not at all clear. Reagan was especially effective at using American strength to support foreign policy, but his military build-up and the strong words he used toward the Soviets increased the danger of war. The United States has given up many international responsibilities in this period, and many U.S. allies criticize America for ignoring their concerns and needs.

In sum, American foreign policy tends to change often, at least in the twentieth century. The goals of the policy shift frequently, and this upsets many of the country's closest allies. The United States is generally hesitant to use its strength, but President Truman relied on American economic strength, and President Reagan stressed military strength. America has always found it hard to cooperate with other countries. The United States is too accustomed to carrying out its own policy.

THE STYLE OF AMERICAN FOREIGN POLICY

The American experience of growing up as a nation is quite unique and has had an important impact on foreign policy. The United States and the entire continent of North America developed in isolation from Europe. Americans felt that they had a special mission in the world. It was called "manifest destiny," meaning that somehow God had favored them, and the United States was the *best* country. The European states had to make adjustments constantly because of their neighboring countries, but America did not have any threatening neighbors.

American foreign policy-makers have never been

accustomed to bargaining with other countries to design American policy. In the 1970s, however, the limits to American policy and the importance of some of our allies, including Japan and West Germany became unmistakably visible. James Schlesinger, a former secretary of defense, describes how the picture of the United States has become very negative:

> Since 1975 . . . the image of the United States, powerful, possessing national unity, and steady in its foreign policy objectives, has given way to a perception of the United States as divided, erratic, and unpredictable, plagued by an eighteenth century constitution, and occasionally provincial.

Americans generally feel that U.S. policies are for the good of the rest of the world, but other countries sometimes resent the United States for telling them what to do.

The search for solutions. American foreign policy has always been very practical about solving problems. The people assume that the normal situation for international relations is to have harmony and stability. If something blocks the stability, then it should be removed. The emphasis in American foreign policy, therefore, is on "trouble avoidance." Crises happen, but the American belief is that they should be handled quickly so that the natural harmony can return. Americans expect that reasonable people can always sit down together and find a reasonable solution to a problem. If the other side does not agree with the American proposals, the American people grow impatient and dissatisfied.

This picture of a stable, harmonious world may not

be accurate. It may be that the normal situation for international affairs is to have a continuous series of conflicts and crises. Perhaps there is no single answer to a foreign policy problem. Everyone may need to give in a little. But this has never been the long-range American approach. The Americans still prefer a quick rescue operation over a long bargaining process.

In this book, we have often talked about the wish of the United States to be a model democracy for the world. We can call this American **moralism** because Americans felt that we could show everyone else how to run their countries. The American political environment (or culture) has put heavy emphasis on this moralism, on the uniqueness and isolationism of the country, and on the desire to solve problems quickly.

These American traditions have served the country well. There is nothing wrong with them, but they may not be the best guides to foreign policy in the last years of the twentieth century. Americans consciously chose two hundred years ago not to centralize power in our government. The decision was that some efficiency could be sacrificed to guarantee a more democratic way to make decisions.

The question is whether the United States can still afford to have an inefficient foreign policy in this way. The problems in the world are quite different today than they were even twenty or thirty years ago. Problems having to do with the oceans, the environment, drugs, food, outer space, and comunications are all part of foreign policy, and individual countries cannot solve the problems alone. The countries are locked together by one another's problems; the problems and the solutions need to be interrelated. We call this **interdependence.**

Like other countries, America must deal with this interdependence. Solutions have to be found that balance everyone's needs. No one denies that the United States is still the most powerful country in the world, but other countries have increased their relative importance in the world in recent years. As a result, America should be more willing to listen to the needs of these other countries. The United States has not become weak or ordinary, but it does have to listen more carefully to the rest of the world.

Rather than trying to force U.S. solutions on international relations, America should aim to "manage" its foreign policy better. While Henry Kissinger was secretary of state, he talked about the *new international system*. He said, "Gone is the rigid bipolar confrontation of the Cold War. In its place is a more fluid and complex world—with many centers of power, more subtle dangers, and new hopeful opportunities." The challenge for American foreign policy is to concentrate on the new hopeful opportunities.

THE TWILIGHT OF INTERNATIONALISM?

During the 1970s Americans worried about whether the county was becoming weak and losing its importance in the world. Today, there is a different concern: Is America losing its interest in international issues? Is the sun setting on the days of American international cooperation? These developments have been described as the *twilight of internationalism* in the United States, and they should cause some concern.

Figure 22 An American fills up his Japanese-made Toyota car with OPEC gas. The increasing dependence of the U.S. on other countries has complicated foreign policy decisions.

The criticism. American foreign policy since 1945 has stressed ways of expanding international cooperation, but President Reagan has not followed this rule. Congressman Lee Hamilton has said the following:

> Diplomacy and negotiations are out of fashion for many U.S. policymakers these days. The United States often prefers to define problems in ways that permit America to deal with them on its own—without negotiations, without asking or listening to others, without dwelling on the consequences of these actions in an interdependent world, and without asking whether U.S. action is the best way to resolve the foreign policy problems.

The Congressman compliments President Reagan

elsewhere for restoring the image of American power. Americans feel good about themselves again. But the Congressman also criticizes the president for not using American power to shape international agreements that protect U.S. interests.

In the trouble spots for U.S. foreign policy—the Middle East, Central America, Southern Africa, arms control—the United States has not had much diplomatic success in the 1980s. Also, the country has worked against some already existing international agreements. America walked away from the Law of the Sea Treaty, it says it will not accept decisions of the International Court of Justice, and the United States withdrew its membership and financial support from UNESCO (the United Nations Educational, Scientific, and Cultural Organization). Of course there are explanations for these steps, but when other countries see the steps, they wonder about America's international commitment. They also worry about U.S. policy, which sometimes does not seem to take arms control seriously and which announces the massive SDI (Strategic Defense Initiative—also called "Star Wars") program without talking to any other countries.

The answer of the Reagan Administration. In fairness to members of the Reagan Administration, they would draw different conclusions. They would emphasize the rebuilding of U.S. military power and the recovery of the American economy that has taken place. The Reagan Administration points with pride to the increases in the number of democratic countries and free market economies in the 1980s. According to the Administration, America's economic success with decentralizing and deregulating has encouraged countries such as India, Yugoslavia, and Brazil to copy the U.S. model.

President Reagan says that he does not measure foreign policy success according to the number of agreements signed. He says that his policy has been successful because the people are proud of their country and there is a consensus that the United States should play an active role in the world. The Reagan Administration has given notice to the world that it will work hard to stop terrorism and the sale of drugs. And the Reagan Administration feels that it has helped push the Philippines, Pakistan, Haiti, and other countries toward democracy.

What drives American foreign policy? The dilemmas which we see in American foreign policy reflect the same issues which have been evident for two centuries. The mood of the United States swings from wanting to be active in foreign policy to wanting to be minimally involved. One way to describe this is to say that America swings from periods of missionary zeal, when we want to use our good will and energy to reshape the world, to periods of withdrawal. For the most part, though, the bad experiences of the 1930s cured Americans from wanting total isolation. Now the question is how active the country should be in its foreign policy.

To the question about the "twilight of internationalism," we can best answer by saying that American foreign policy has always been burdened with conflicting tendencies. If people are correct that the United States is less involved internationally today, then this too will probably swing the other direction in a few years. That does not mean that the problem is unimportant, but it does mean that the shifts away from internationalism are probably not permanent.

CAN WE COMBINE REALISM AND VISION IN AMERICAN FOREIGN POLICY?

What are the alternatives for future U.S. foreign policy? We can identify the swings in mood, but does that help us design the policy for years to come? James Billington, a Soviet expert and the recently named librarian of congress, argues that there has been a historic clash in American foreign policy since World War II between visions and reality. He says that U.S. foreign policy needs to combine these two schools of thought if it is to be successful and effective in the future.

In late 1986 Americans were shocked by the news of secret arms sales to Iran and the illegal transfer of money to the U.S.-backed freedom fighters ("Contras") in Nicaragua. The Contras were trying to overthrow the Communist-backed government in Nicaragua. Foreign policy seemed to be in a mess. But foreign policy is too important to be a spectator sport. The policy has to be related to some sense of America's place in the world. Unfortunately, the United States has not been certain how it should relate to a changing world ever since the consensus on foreign policy broke apart during the Vietnam War.

Billington looks at the split personality of the American foreign policy community, and asks how can we bring the two sides together. He compares those who want to base foreign policy on short-term reality with those who want to base it on long-term ideal visions.

The view based on short-term reality. This view sees U.S. involvement in the world as a negative reaction to the threat of the Soviet Union. To balance this threat, the United States needs military strength to contain the Soviets and a strong network of alliances to reinforce the American position. This **realist-conservative view** favors a continuation of the U.S. military build-up and an aggressive push in high technology to increase the advantage of the West over the East.

The view based on long-term ideal visions. This view sees U.S. involvement in the world as a positive result of the dynamic American political and economic system. America needs to continue to be a model for the rest of the world and support the worldwide spread of democracy. The Soviets pose a military and political threat, but the threat is only secondary in importance. The real issues are global problems such as ignorance, poverty, and pollution. In the short run, the United States should focus on helping the less developed countries that are starting to move toward democracy. This is the **idealist-liberal view.**

Combining the realist and idealist views. In some ways these views correspond to the thinking of Republican and Democratic administrations in the past twenty-five to thirty years, but that is an oversimplification. A liberal president like John Kennedy was willing to take a hard line with the Soviets, and a conservative president like Ronald Reagan also focuses on global democratization and the abolition of nuclear weapons. The most serious issue, though, is deciding whether these two views necessarily conflict. The realist-conservative view suggests that America has to stand ready to deal decisively with short-term problems; the idealist-liberal view describes the way Americans see themselves ideally in the long-range future. Billington argues that there is nothing wrong with recognizing the short-run need for a Cold War and the long-run need for a freer, more prosperous earth.

If a policy-maker pays attention only to the realism of the first view, he emphasizes the need for military strength. This, however, is not enough, according to Billington. Making weapons should not be the main focus of foreign policy. The vision of the second view needs to be added to the realism of the first view. The democratic experiment has always needed both a strong defense for protection and a guiding idea to carry to the rest of the world. The international obligation of the United States is not only to build up the military; it involves higher aims, and the programs to deal with world poverty or ignorance have to be a central part of the American foreign policy plan. This may not be easy for the United States because it will involve sacrifices and some sharing of American wealth, but in the long run the entire world would benefit.

In conclusion, the task for future American foreign policy is to (1) maintain the democratic traditions of the past and (2) combine a realistic short-term foreign policy of strength with a longer-term vision. The world is changing so fast that new possibilities of cooperation arise constantly. Cooperation does not mean that no conflict exists between countries, but it does involve nations working together to decide what their goals are for the world.

On the one hand, no country has done as good a job as the United States in keeping a vision in mind in its foreign policy. On the other hand, the United States has never been very successful in cooperating with other countries to make foreign policy. The American tendency to let foreign policy be decided democratically has sometimes caused our policy to be inefficient. Still, America must maintain this democratic approach and try, at the same time, to cooperate more effectively with other countries. This is the challenge for the future. As the leaders of tomorrow, you will decide how we will meet this difficult challenge. If we can interact with other countries while remaining faithful to our national traditions, we will have a promising future to look forward to.

REVIEW QUESTIONS

1. Tocqueville says that democracies are "inferior" in making foreign policy. Is that fair?
2. Are American presidents well prepared to make foreign policy?
3. The American public plays an important role in making foreign policy. Is it easier or harder for a democratic country like the United States to make a clear foreign policy? Why?

4. Is America becoming less interested in international cooperation?
5. Is the United States generous with foreign assistance to other countries?
6. How can the United States combine realism and vision in its foreign policy? Should more emphasis be placed on military security or on dealing with problems such as ignorance, poverty, and pollution?

APPENDICES

THE AMERICAN CIVIC ANIMAL

In this section we will introduce some of the people who are actually involved with this issue. You will find out how you can get more information about the issue and how you can get involved yourself. You will also be introduced to a wise and friendly beast, a cool creature: The American Civic Animal. . . .

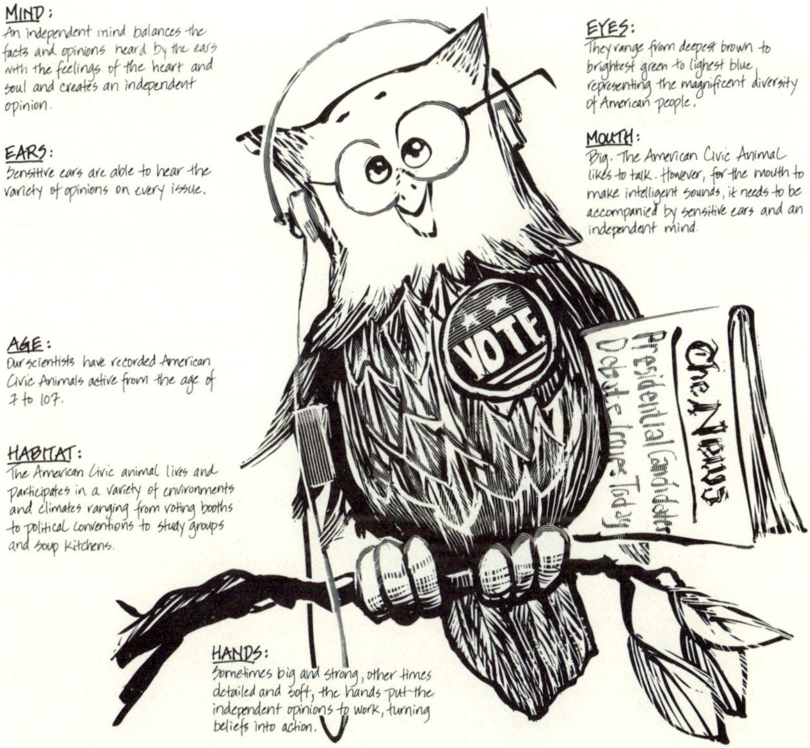
MIND:
An independent mind balances the facts and opinions heard by the ears with the feelings of the heart and soul and creates an independent opinion.
EARS:
Sensitive ears are able to hear the variety of opinions on every issue.
EYES:
They range from deepest brown to brightest green to lighest blue, representing the magnificent diversity of American people.
MOUTH:
Big. The American Civic Animal likes to talk. However, for the mouth to make intelligent sounds, it needs to be accompanied by sensitive ears and an independent mind.
VOTE
The News
Presidential Candidates
Debate Times Today
AGE:
Our scientists have recorded American Civic Animals active from the age of 7 to 107.
HABITAT:
The American Civic animal lives and participates in a variety of environments and climates ranging from voting booths to political conventions to study groups and soup kitchens.
HANDS:
Sometimes big and strong, other times detailed and soft, the hands put the independent opinions to work, turning beliefs into action.

Activities:

Voting, reading, listening, organizing, demonstrating. It's quite difficult to narrow down just what American Civic Animals do. They are often spotted writing or calling their Congresspersons and representatives to keep these elected officials informed about what they feel. They have been sighted organizing summer activities for underprivileged youth and cooking meals for Senior Citizens who have trouble shopping for themselves. Perhaps you have seen American Civic Animals passing out leaflets at shopping malls, or singing songs at rallies. There are as many ways to participate as there are issues that need attention, and Americans eager to be involved. In the final examination, there is one trait that all American Civic Animals share:

American Civic Animals keep informed!

They often consume newspapers. Favorite national papers include the *New York Times,* the *Washington Post,* the *Los Angeles Times* and *USA Today* among others. Local papers also offer a wealth of regional information. American Civic Animals listen to television and radio news programs. In addition, they listen and talk with parents, teachers, coaches, sisters, brothers, neighbors and friends. Because without listening, learning and exchanging ideas, American Civic Animals can not wisely engage in one of their most fundamental and important activities: voting. If they can not keep informed, get involved or vote, they can not stay free. In a letter from one great American Civic Animal, Thomas Jefferson, to another great American Civic Animal, John Adams, Jefferson summed it up: "If a nation expects to be ignorant and free . . . it expects what never was and never will be." The American Civic Animal realizes that one can not be ignorant and free. The American Civic Animal gets involved first by keeping informed.

American Civic Animals are also joiners:

Observing the American Civil Animal 150 years ago, French author and traveller Alexis de Tocqueville said, "Americans of all ages, all stations of life, and all types of disposition are forever forming associations . . . of a thousand different types—religious, moral, serious, futile, very general and very limited, immensely large and very minute . . . At the head of any new undertaking, where in France you would find the government or in England some territorial magnate, in the United States you are sure to find an association." The American Civic Animals of today are just as apt to join organizations and associations as they were in de Tocqueville's time.

American Civil Animals often work with national organizations, but they also like to quench their thirst for involvement in a number of community oriented ways—such as neighborhood crime prevention groups, school support organizations, or environmental education programs.

The first step in becoming an American Civic Animal is to keep informed by reading a newspaper, reading a newsmagazine or listening to the television or radio news programs. What if you want more information? What if you want to become even more involved? The following sections will give you some specific next steps and some specific organizations.

HOW TO START

- Find the correct organization or individual: if you are interested in addressing the issue of poverty in America, the Foreign Policy Association probably would not be the best organization for you to contact. Similarly, if you want to let your Senator know what you feel about a balanced Federal Budget, for example, you must know his/her name. The best place to find out the correct organization and/or name is in your local or school library. The Book of Associations, which is usually in the reference section of a library, lists thousands of organizations and associations that deal with many different issues. Often the librarian can help you choose which one is appropriate for you. To find out the name of your Congressperson or Senator, one easy way to do it, is to call the Capitol switchboard in Washington, D.C. at (202) 224-3121. If no one you know can tell you the correct name, the operator who answers this number will.

- Find the correct address or telephone number. After you have found the appropriate organization or individual, you need to contact them. This can be done either in writing or by phone. (Remember: Calling is more expensive than writing!) If the organization is local, check your local phone book. If it is outside your area, check for the telephone number and address in the Book of Associations. If you don't know the address or the telephone number, but you do know the town or city that the organization is in, call the area code for that city and then 555-1212. Tell the operator the city and the name of the organization and he/she will give you the correct telephone number. All members of Congress can be phoned by calling the Capitol switchboard at the number listed in the paragraphs above.
- Write or call. Many organizations and elected officials are pleased to hear from interested people. Many are eager to pass out information or to get help from energetic volunteers who care about the issues they deal with. Many organizations, including both political parties and a citizens' action groups, welcome your participation. After keeping informed, getting involved is the next step to becoming an American Civic Animal.
- What happens then? If you're calling or writing for information, ask for the specific type you are looking for. If you want to get involved with the organization,

it's best if you tell them you would like to volunteer your services. Very few organizations can afford to pay their young employees, although some organizations do. Most organizations will allow flexible hours to allow for school or other employment. What you end up doing depends on the organization. You might be speaking with people on the phone; you might write letters; you might deliver meals or translate languages. While the work is not always thrilling, being involved in an issue you care about and seeing the difference you make can be very exciting. And that can be a lot of fun. The next section describes some organizations that deal with the specific issues addressed in this book.

RESOURCES

The Foreign Policy Association

Since 1918 The Foreign Policy Association has kept Americans informed about foreign policy issues in creative and innovative ways. FPA, a very good source for non-partisan information on foreign affairs, sponsors exciting educational programs throughout the country. It may seem unusual to see a sixteen-year-old arguing with her school principal about foreign policy, but for a number of schools participating in FPA's educational projects, student-teacher and student-principal foreign policy discussions are only the beginning. FPA selects ten important foreign affairs questions each year. The topics for 1987 included: "The Constitution and Foreign Policy"; "South Africa"; and "Dealing with Revolution: Iran, Nicaragua and the Philippines." FPA then produces school curricula, radio programs, and television shows which focus on these issues. In addition, FPA also sponsors "Student Town Meetings" where hundreds of students are invited to watch and participate in a panel discussion on a specific topic. In 1986 the Atlanta "Student Town Meeting" featured a panel which included students and former President Jimmy Carter; The New York "Student Town Meeting's" panel featured New York area students and former Secretary of State Alexander Haig. FPA also sponsors a "Think International Essay Contest" for students from all over the country. In 1986, the twenty-nine high school student winners were flown to New York City for a luncheon with Secretary of State George Schultz.

If you are interested in learning more about the Foreign Policy Association and its offerings, write or call:

The Foreign Policy Association
205 Lexington Avenue
New York, NY 10016
(212) 481-8450

Friends Committee on National Legislation

Do you ever wonder exactly what your Congresspersons are doing? We all hear about the important ideas being debated, but what legislation is actually being passed and defeated? If you want to keep updated on what is happening in the halls of Congress, the Friends Committee on National Legislation Washington Newsletter is a terrific resource. With the historically pro-peace perspective of the Quaker church ("Friends" is another name for Quaker), the Washington Newsletter reviews and analyzes the important pieces of legislation being considered at any one time. In addition, the Friends Committee compiles a tape daily, in order to keep you updated on the happenings on Capitol Hill. That phone number is (202) 547-4343. If you are interested in learning more about the Friends Committee, or in subscribing to the Newsletter for your family or for your school write:

Friends Committee on National Legislation
245 Second Street, N.E.
Washington, D.C. 20002

American Enterprise Institute

"Competition of ideas is fundamental to a free society." The American Enterprise Institute produces ideas, competing ideas. AEI does not lobby Congress. AEI does not assist grassroots organizations. AEI does not follow any particular political ideology. That doesn't mean that AEI isn't political. Often called a "think tank" or "idea factory," the Institute sponsors the research of scholars in a wide range of areas. These scholars, experts in fields ranging from *Human Rights and Race* to *Agriculture Policy* meet together with members of Congress, policymakers, business and labor leaders, as well as with themselves, to discuss policy ideas. The scholars then write educational and academic papers which AEI publishes.

Although AEI is "nonpartisan" it openly supports "a liberal economic order," or *private enterprise,* and the *military strength* necessary to defend and promote our economic order. The head of AEI's Foreign Policy and Defense Studies, Jeane J. Kirkpatrick, served as U.S. Ambassador to the United Nations under President Reagan. The research she has written for AEI, like the work she did as Ambassador, supports a strong nuclear defense as the best way to ensure peace with the Soviet Union. If you would like to learn more about how "think tanks," such as AEI, work, or if you would like to find out more about AEI ideas, write:

American Enterprise Institute
1150 17th Street, N.W.
Washington, D.C. 20036

The United Nations Association of the United States (UNA/USA)

The United Nations is more than debates and resolutions. It can be a means for governments to work together to deal with problems that touch everyone's life: the spread of nuclear arms, world economics, environmental pollution, oppression, and injustice. The United Nations Association of the United States, chaired by former Secretary of Defense Elliot Richardson, former Secretary of State Cyrus Vance, and past President of the League of Women Voters, Ruth Hinerfeld, is a link between the United Nations and you. The organization's goal is to help make the United Nations more effective.

The UNA/USA keeps its members informed about the happenings at the United Nations and other international organizations. In addition, the UNA/USA uses members' input to prepare policy recommendations on various topics. Their bimonthly newspapers and numerous position papers are helpful tools for anyone wishing to keep informed. If you are interested in joining the UNA/USA write:

The United Nations Association of the U.S.A.
485 Fifth Avenue
New York, NY 10017-6104

The Experiment in International Living

Since its founding in 1932, the Experiment in International Living (EIL) has been a leader in international education and exchange. The Experiment's goal is to educate people for life in an *interdependent* world. All of their programs help people to "understand—take action—and care about—the well being of our common planet." Foreign affairs issues come to life when one lives with a family in a foreign country, or when your family opens its home to an international visitor.

The oldest organization of its kind in the world, The Experiment invented the homestay concept of learning the culture of another country by living as a member of one of its families. Today, homestays are only one part of the Experiment's program. The Experiment's School for International Training, in Battleboro, Vermont, offers undergraduate and graduate degrees in international studies and foreign languages. Throughout the United States, Experiment language training sites offer intensive English lessons for international citizens from around the world. The organization is also involved in overseas development projects. Working in collaboration with Save the Children

Federation and World Education, the Experiment helped prepare more than 70,000 Indochinese refugees in English language, cross-cultural and prevocational skills prior to their relocation to the United States.

If you would like information about the Experiment's programs, including the summer abroad homestays (scholarships are available based on need and personal qualifications) write:

The Experiment in International Living
Kipling Road
Battleboro, Vermont 05301

SANE

Do you want to study foreign policy issues from a propeace perspective? Do you want to get actively involved in the Peace Movement? If you answer yes to either of these questions, you should contact SANE.

SANE believes that military spending is wasteful; that the development of faster and more accurate nuclear weapons threatens the safety of our planet; that the money spent on bombs and missiles would be better spent fighting poverty and improving American education. For three decades, SANE has supported these beliefs by educating citizens, lobbying Congresspersons, researching arms issues, and supporting propeace candidates. SANE's one-hundred-fifty-thousand members work on both a grassroots and national level. Grassroots efforts include door-to-door canvassing and recruiting. ("Canvassers" walk from house to house, talking with people about arms race issues, handing out literature, and answering questions. SANE canvassers talk to people in 20,000 homes each week.) Nationally, SANE sponsors public hearings, the SANE magazine, *SANE World*, and a weekly radio program, "Consider the Alternatives."

SANE welcomes youth involvement. If you would like to look at their research and educational materials, find out how your congressional representatives have voted on peace issues, or actually volunteer for SANE, write:

SANE
711 G Street, S.E.
Washington, D.C. 20003

Apartheid:

Apartheid and the human rights violations of the government of South Africa have fueled indignation and protest all across the globe. How the United States government deals with South Africa is one foreign policy issue of grave concern for many Americans. If you are interested in learning more about the various sides to the South Africa issue, the Foreign Policy Association (highlighted above) would be a good resource.

Two organizations taking a strong stand against Apartheid are the NAACP and PUSH. Both the NAACP, the eighty-year-old National Association for the Advancement of Colored People, and PUSH, Rev. Jesse Jackson's People United to Save Humanity, can be valuable sources for information. In addition, PUSH and the NAACP encourage youth involvement in the anti-Apartheid movement. If you would like to learn more about the anti-Apartheid movement, call or write:

PUSH
P. O. Box 5432
Chicago, IL
60680-9919

NAACP
4805 Mt. Hope Drive
Baltimore, Md.
21215

Youth Groups

Do you want to learn about a number of foreign policy issues ranging from the arms race to Apartheid to terrorism to world economic problems? Do you want to take a stand and get involved in any of these issues? Do other concerns such as civil rights, world hunger, pollution, and poverty interest you? Perhaps you should join a youth group in your community. Synagogues, churches, the Boy Scouts, and the Girl Scouts are just a few of the organizations sponsoring active youth groups in your neighborhood. Through these groups you can participate in a number of these important issues. Youth groups are also a great place to find friends and meet supportive adult sponsors who want you to get involved. Give them a try!

FEDERALIST PAPER NO. 51: JAMES MADISON

To what expedient, then, shall we finally resort, for maintaining in practice the necessary partition of power among the several departments as laid down in the Constitution? The only answer that can be given is that as all these exterior provisions are found to be inadequate the defect must be supplied, by so contriving the interior structure of the government as that its several constituent parts may, by their mutal relations, be the means of keeping each other in their proper places. Without presuming to undertake a full development of this important idea I will hazard a few general observations which may perhaps place it in a clearer light, and enable us to form a more correct judgment of the principles and structure of the government planned by the convention.

In order to lay a due foundation for that separate and distinct exercise of the different powers of government, which to a certain extent is admitted on all hands to be essential to the preservation of liberty, it is evident that each department should have a will of its own; and consequently should be so constituted that the members of each should have as little agency as possible in the appointment of the members of the others. Were this principle rigorously adhered to, it would require that all the appointments for the supreme executive, legislative and judiciary magistracies should be drawn from the same fountain of authority, the people, through channels having no communication whatever with one another. Perhaps such a plan of constructing the several departments would be less difficult in practice than it may in contemplation appear. Some difficulties, however, and some additional expenses would attend the execution of it. Some deviations, therefore, from the principle must be admitted. In the constitution of the judiciary department in particular, it might be inexpedient to insist rigorously on this principle: first, because peculiar qualifications being essential in the members, the primary consideration ought to be to select that mode of choice which best secures those qualifications; second, because the permanent tenure by which the appointments are held in that department must soon destroy all sense of dependence on the authority conferring them.

It is equally evident that the members of each department should be as little dependent as possible on those of the others for the emoluments annexed to their offices. Were the executive magistrate, or the judges, not independent of the legislature in this particular, their independence in every other would be merely nominal.

But the great security against a gradual concentration of the several powers in the same department consists in giving to those who administer each department the necessary constitutive means and personal motives to resist encroachments of the others. The provision for defense must in this, as in all other cases, be made commensurate to the danger of attack. Ambition must be made to counteract ambition. The interest of the man must be connected with the constitutional rights of the place. It may be a reflection on human nature that such devices should be necessary to control the abuses of government. But what is government itself but the greatest of all reflections on human nature? If men were angels, no government would be necessary. If angels were to govern men, neither external nor internal controls on government would be necessary. In framing a government which is to be administered by and over men, the greatest difficulty lies in this: you must first enable the government to control the governed; and in the next place oblige it to control itself. A dependence on the people is, no doubt, the primary control on the government; but experience has taught mankind the necessity of auxiliary precautions.

This policy of supplying, by opposite and rival interests, the defect of better motives, might be traced through the whole system of human affairs, private as well as public. We see it particularly displayed in all the subordinate distributions of power, where the constant aim is to divide and arrange the several offices in such a way that each may be a check on the other—that the private interest of every individual may be a sentinel over the public rights. These inventions of prudence cannot be less requisite in the distribution of the supreme powers of the State.

But it is not possible to give to each department an equal power of self-defense. In republican government the legislative authority necessarily predominates. The remedy for this inconveniency is to divide the legislature into different branches; and to render them, by different modes of election and different principles of action, as little connected with each other as the nature of their common functions and their common dependence on the society will admit. It may even be necessary to guard against dangerous encroachments by still further precautions. As the weight of the legislative authority requires that it should be thus divided, the weakness of the executive may require, on the other hand, that it should be fortified. An absolute negative on the legislature appears, at first, to be the natural defense with which the executive magistrate should be armed. But perhaps it would be neither altogether safe nor alone sufficient. On ordinary occasions it might not be exerted with the requisite firmness, and on extraordinary occasions it might be perfidiously abused. May not this defect of an absolute negative be supplied by some qualified connection between this weaker department and the weaker branch of the stronger department, by which the latter may be led to support the constitutional rights of the former, without being too much detached from the rights of its own department?

If the principles on which these observations are founded be just, as I persuade myself they are, and they be applied as a criterion to the several State constitutions, and to the federal Constitution, it will be found that if the latter does not perfectly correspond with them, the former are infinitely less able to bear such a test.

There are, moreover, two considerations particularly applicable to the federal system of America, which place that system in a very interesting point of view.

First. In a single republic, all the power surrendered by the people is submitted to the administration of a single government; and the usurpations are guarded against by a division of the government into distinct and separate departments. In the compound republic of America, the power surrendered by the people is first divided between two distinct governments, and then the portion allotted to each subdivided among distinct and separate departments. Hence a double security arises to the rights of the people. The different governments will control each other, at the same time that each will be controlled by itself.

Second. It is of great importance in a republic not only to guard the society against the oppression of its rulers, but to guard one part of the society against the injustice of the other part. Different interests necessarily exist in different classes of citizens. If a majority be united in a common interest, the rights of the minority will be insecure. There are but two methods of providing against this evil: the one by creating a will in the community independent of the majority—that is, of the society itself; the other, by comprehending in the society so many separate descriptions of citizens as will render an unjust combination of the majority of the whole very improbable, if not impracticable. The first method prevails in all governments possessing an hereditary or self-appointed authority. This, at best, is but a precarious security; because a power independent of the society may as well espouse the unjust views of the major as well as the rightful interests of the minor party, and may possibly be turned against both parties. The second method will be exemplified in the federal republic of the United States. Whilst all authority in it will be derived from and dependent on the society, the society itself will be broken into so many parts, interests, and classes of citizens, that the rights of individuals, or of the minority, will be in little danger from the interested combinations of the majority. In a free government the security for civil rights must be the same as that for religious rights. It consists in the one case in the multiplicity of interests, and in the other in the multiplicity of sects. The degree of security in both cases will depend on the number of interests and sects; and this may be presumed to depend on the extent of country and number of people comprehended under the same government. This view of the subject must particularly recommend a proper federal system to all the sincere and considerate friends of republican government, since it shows that in exact proportion as the territory of the Union may be formed into more circumscribed Confederacies, or States, oppressive combinations of a majority will be facilitated; the best security, under the republican forms, for the rights of every class of citizen, will be diminished; and consequently the stability and independence of some member of the government, the only other security, must be proportionally increased. Justice is the end of government. It is the end of civil society. It ever has been and ever will be pursued until it be obtained, or until liberty be lost in the pursuit. In a society under the forms of which the stronger faction can readily unite and oppress the weaker, anarchy may as truly be said to reign as in the state of nature, where the weaker individual is not secured against the violence of the stronger; and as, in the latter state, even the stronger individuals are prompted, by the uncertainty of their condition, to submit to a government which may protect the weak as well as themselves; so, in the former state, will the more powerful factions or parties be gradually induced, by a like motive, to wish for a government which will protect all parties, the weaker as well as the more powerful. It can be little doubted that if the State of Rhode Island was separated from the Confederacy and left to itself, the insecurity of rights under the popular form of government within such narrow limits would be displayed by such reiterated oppressions of factious majorities that some power altogether independent of the people would soon be called for by the voice of the very factions whose misrule had proved the necessity of it. In the extended republic of the United States, and among the great variety of interests, parties, and sects which it embraces, a coalition of a majority of the whole society could seldom take place on any other principles than those of justice and the general good; whilst there being thus less danger to a minor from the will of a major party, there must be less pretext, also, to provide for the security of the former, by introducing into the government a will not dependent on the latter, or, in other words, a will independent of the society itself. It is no less certain that it is important, notwithstanding the contrary opinions which have been entertained, that the larger the society, provided it lie within a practicable sphere, the more duly capable it will be of self-government. And happily for the republican cause, the practicable sphere may be carried to a very great extent by a judicious modification and mixture of the federal principle.

—Publius

A precise knowledge of our relations with foreign powers as respects our negotiation with each is thought to be particularly necessary. . . .

At the proposal of the Russian Imperial government, made through the minister of the emperor residing here, full power and instructions have been transmitted to the minister of the United States at St. Petersburg to arrange by amicable negotiation the respective rights and interests of the two nations on the northwest coast of this continent. A similar proposal had been made by His Imperial Majesty to the Government of Great Britain, which has likewise been acceded to. The government of the United States has been desirous, by this friendly proceeding, of manifesting the great value which they have invariably attached to the friendship of the emperor and their solicitude to cultivate the best understanding with his government.

In the discussions to which this interest has given rise and in the arrangements by which they may terminate the occasion has been judged proper for asserting, as a principle in which the rights and interests of the United States are involved, that the American continents, by the free and independent condition which they have assumed and maintain, are henceforth not to be considered as subjects for future colonization by any European powers. . . .

It was stated at the commencement of the last session that great effort was then making in Spain and Portugal to improve the condition of the people of those countries and that it appeared to be conducted with extraordinary moderation. It need scarcely be remarked that the result has been so far very different from what was then anticipated. Of events in that quarter of the globe with which we have so much intercourse and from which we derive our origin, we have always been anxious and interested spectators. The citizens of the United States cherish sentiments the most friendly in favor of the liberty and happiness of their fellowmen on that side of the Atlantic. In the wars of the European powers in matters relating to themselves we have never taken any part, nor does it comport with our policy to do so. It is only when our rights are invaded or seriously menaced that we resent injuries or make preparation for our defense.

With the movements in this hemisphere we are of necessity more immediately connected,and by causes which must be obvious to all enlightened and impartial observers. The political system of the allied powers is essentially different in this respect from that of America. This difference proceeds from that which exists in their respective governments; and to the defense of our own, which has been achieved by the loss of so much blood and treasure, and matured by the wisdom of their most enlightened citizens, and under which we have enjoyed unexampled felicity, this whole nation is devoted. We owe it, therefore, to candor and to the amicable relations existing between the United States and those powers to declare that we should consider any attempt on their part to extend their system to any portion of this hemisphere as dangerous to our peace and safety.

With the existing colonies or dependencies of any European power we have not interfered and shall not interfere. But with the governments who have declared their independence and maintained it, and whose independence we have, on great consideration and on just principles, acknowledged, we could not view any interposition for the purpose of oppressing them, or controlling in any other manner their destiny, by any European power in any other light than as the manifestation of an unfriendly disposition toward the United States. In the war between those new governments and Spain we declared our neutrality at the time of their recognition, and to this we have adhered, and shall continue to adhere, provided no change shall occur which, in the judgment of the competent authorities of this government, shall make a corresponding change on the part of the United States indispensable to their security.

The late events in Spain and Portugal show that Europe is still unsettled. Of this important fact no stronger proof can be adduced than that the allied powers should have thought it proper, on any principle satisfactory to themselves, to have interposed by force in the internal concerns of Spain. To what extent such interposition may be carried, on the same principle, is a question in which all independent powers whose governments differ from theirs are interested, even those most remote, and surely none more so than the United States.

Our policy in regard to Europe, which was adopted at an early stage of the wars which have so long agitated that quarter of the globe, nevertheless remains the same, which is not to interfere in the internal concerns of any of its powers; to consider the government de facto as the legitimate government for us; to cultivate friendly relations with it, and to preserve those relations by a frank, firm, and manly policy, meeting in all instances the just claims of every power, submitting to injuries from none. But in regard to those continents, circumstances are eminently and conspicuously different. It is impossible that the allied powers should extend their political system to any portion of either continent without endangering our peace and happiness; nor can anyone believe that our southern brethern, if left to themsleves, would adopt it of their own accord.

It is equally impossible, therefore, that we should behold such interposition in any form with indifference. If we look to the comparative strength and resources of Spain and those new governments, and their distance from each other, it must be obvious that she can never subdue them. It is still the true policy of the United States to leave the parties to themselves, in the hope that other powers will pursure the same course.

WINSTON CHURCHILL: THE IRON CURTAIN

Neither the sure prevention of war nor the continuous rise of world organization will be gained without what I have called the fraternal organization of the English-speaking peoples. This means a special relationship between the British Commonwealth and Empire and the United States.

This is no time for generalities. I will venture to be precise. Fraternal association requires not only the growing friendship and mutual understanding between our two vast but kindred systems of society but the continuance of the intimate relationships between our military advisers, leading to common study of potential dangers, similarity of weapons and manuals of instruction, and interchange of officers and cadets at colleges. It should carry with it the continuance of the present facilities for mutual security by the joint use of all naval and air force bases in the possession of either country all over the world. This would perhaps double the mobility of the American Navy and Air Force. It would greatly expand that of the British Empire forces, and it might well lead, if and as the world calms down, to important financial savings. Already we use together a large number of islands; many more will be entrusted to our joint care in the near future.

The United States already has a permanent defense agreement with the Dominion of Canada, which is so devotedly attached to the British Commonwealth and Empire. This agreement is more effective than many of those which have often been made under formal alliances. This principle should be extended to all the British commonwealths with full reciprocity. Thus, whatever happens, and thus only we shall be secure ourselves and able to work together for the high and simple causes that are dear to us and bode no ill to any. Eventually there may come the principle of common citizenship, but that we may be content to leave to destiny, whose outstretched arm so many of us can clearly see.

There is, however, an important question we must ask ourselves. Would a special relationship between the United States and the British Commonwealth be inconsistent with our overriding loyalties to the world organization? I reply that, on the contrary, it is probably the only means by which the organization will achieve its full stature and strength. There are already the special United States relations with Canada and between the United States and the South American republics. We also have our twenty-year treaty of collaboration and mutual assistance with Soviet Russia. I agree with Mr. Bevin that it might well be a fifteen-year treaty. We have an alliance with Portugal unbroken since 1384. None of these clash with the general interest of a world agreement. On the contrary, they help it. "In my father's house are many mansions." Special associations between members of the United Nations which have no aggressive point against any other country, which harbor no design incompatible with the Charter of the United Nations, are beneficial and, as I believe, indispensable.

I spoke earlier of the temple of peace. Workmen from all countries must build that temple. If two of the workmen know each other particularly well and are old friends, if their families are intermingled and if they have faith in each other's purpose, hope in each other's future, and charity toward each other's shortcomings, to quote some good words I read here the other day, why cannot they work together at the common task as friends and partners? Why cannot they share their tools and thus increase each other's working powers? Indeed, they must do so or else the temple may not be built, or, being built, it may collapse, and we shall all be proved unteachable and have to go and try to learn again for a third time, in a school of war, incomparably more rigorous than that from which we have just been released. The Dark Ages may return, the Stone Age may return on the gleaming wings of science, and what might now shower immeasurable material blessings upon mankind may even bring about its total destruction.

Beware, I say: time may be short. Do not let us take the course of letting events drift along until it is too late. If there is to be a fraternal association of the kind I have described, with all the extra strength and security which both our countries can derive from it, let us make sure that the great fact is known to the world, and that it plays its part in steadying and stabilizing the foundations of peace. Prevention is better than cure.

A shadow has fallen upon the scenes so lately lighted by the Allied victory. Nobody knows what Soviet Russia and its Communist international organization intends to do in the immediate future, or what are the limits, if any, to their expansive and proselytizing tendencies. I have a strong admiration and regard for the valiant Russian people and for my wartime comrade Marshal Stalin. There is sympathy and good will in Britain—and I doubt not here also—toward the peoples of all the Russias and a resolve to persevere through many differences and rebuffs in establishing lasting friendships.

We understand the Russians need to be secure on her western frontiers from all renewal of German aggression. We welcome her to her rightful place among the leading nations of the world. Above all we welcome constant, frequent, and growing contacts between the Russian people and our own people on both sides of the Atlantic. It is my duty, however, to place before you certain facts about the present position in Europe—I am sure I do not wish to, but it is my duty, I feel, to present them to you.

From Stettin in the Baltic to Trieste in the Adriatic, and iron curtain has descended across the Continent. Behind that line lie all the capital of the ancient states of central and eastern Europe. Warsaw, Berlin, Prague, Vienna, Budapest, Belgrade, Bucharest, and Sofia, all these famous cities and the populations around them lie in the Soviet sphere and all are subject in one form or another, not only to Soviet influence but to a very high and increasing measure of control from Moscow. Athens alone, with its immortal glories, is free to decide its future at an election under British, American, and French observation. The Russian-dominated Polish government has been encouraged to make enormous and wrongful inroads upon Germany, and mass explusions of millions of Germans on a scale grievous and undreamed of are now taking place.

The Communist parties, which were very small in all these Eastern states of Europe, have been raised to preeminence and power far beyond their numbers and are seeking everywhere to obtain totalitarian control. Police governments are prevailing in nearly every case, and so far, except in Czechoslovakia, there is no true democracy. Turkey and Persia are both profoundly alarmed and disturbed at the claims which are made upon them and at the pressure being exerted by the Moscow government. An attempt is being made by the Russians in Berlin to build up a quasi-Communist party in their zone of occupied Germany by showing special favors to groups of left-wing German leaders.

At the end of the fighting last June, the American and British armies withdrew westward in accordance with an earlier agreement to a depth, at some points, 150 miles on a front of nearly 400 miles to allow the Russians to occupy this vast expanse of territory which the Western democracies had conquered. If now the Soviet government tries, by separate action, to build up a pro-Communist Germany in their areas, this will cause new serious difficulties in the British and American zones and will give the defeated Germans the power of putting themselves up to auction between the Soviets and Western democracies. Whatever conclusions may be drawn from these facts—and facts they are—this is certainly not the liberated Europe we fought to build up. Nor is it the one which contains the essentials of permanent peace.

The safety of the world, ladies and gentlemen, requires a new unity in Europe from which no nation should be permanently outcast.

It is impossible not to comprehend—twice we have seen them drawn by irresistible forces in time to secure the victory but only after frightful slaughter and devastation have occurred. Twice the United States has had to send millions of its young men to fight a war, but now war can find any nation between dawn and dusk. Surely we should work within the structure of the United Nations and in accordance with our Charter. That is an open course of policy.

In front of the iron curtain which lies across Europe are other causes for anxiety. In Italy the Communist Party is seriously hampered by having to support the Communist-trained Marshall Tito's claims to former Italian territory at the head of the Adriatic. Nevertheless, the future of Italy hangs in the balance. Again one cannot imagine a regenerated Europe without a strong France. All my public life I have worked for a strong France and I never lost faith in her destiny, even in the darkest hours. I will not lose faith now.

However, in a great number of countries, far from the Russian frontiers and throughout the world, Communist fifth columns are established and work in complete unity and absolute obedience to the directions they receive from the Communist center. Except in the British Commonwealth and in the United States, where communism is in its infancy, the Communist parties or fifth columns constitute a growing challenge and peril to Christian civilization. These are somber facts for anyone to have to recite on the morrow of a victory gained by so much splendid comradeship-in-arms and in the cause of freedom and democracy, and we should be most unwise not to face them squarely while time remains.

The outlook is also anxious in the Far East, and especially in Manchuria. The agreement which was made in Yalta, to which I was a party, was extremely favorable to Soviet Russia, but it was made at a time when no one could say that the German war might not extend all through the summer and autumn of 1945 and when the Japanese war was expected to last for a further eighteen months from the end of the German war. In this country you are all so well informed about the Far East, and such devoted freinds of China, that I do not need to expatiate on the situation there.

I have felt bound to portray the shadow which, alike in the West and in the East, falls upon the world. I was a minister at the time of the Versailles Treaty and a close friend of Mr. Lloyd George. I did not myself agree with many things that were done, but I have a very vague impression in my mind of that situation, and I find it painful to contrast it with that which prevails now. In those days there were high hopes and unbounded confidence that the wars were over and the League of Nations would become all-powerful. I do not see or feel the same confidence or even the same hopes in the haggard world at this time.

On the other hand I repulse the idea that a new war is inevitable; still more that it is imminent. It is because I am so sure that our fortunes are in our own hands and that we hold the power to save the future that I feel the duty to speak out now that I have an occasion to do so. I do not believe that Soviet Russia desires war. What they desire is the fruits of war and the indefinite expansion of their power and doctrines. But what we have to consider here today, while time remains, is the permanent prevention of war and the establishment of conditions of freedom and democracy as rapidly as possible in all countries.

Our difficulties and dangers will not be removed by

closing our eyes to them. They will not be removed bymere waiting to see what happens; nor will they be relieved by a policy of appeasement. What is needed is a settlement, and the longer this is delayed the more difficult it will be and the greater our dangers will become. From what I have seen of our Russian friends and allies during the war, I am convinced that there is nothing they admire so much as strength, and there is nothing for which they have less respect than for military weakness. For that reason the old doctrine of a balance of power is unsound. We cannot afford, if we can help it, to work on narrow margins, offering temptations to a trial of strength.

If the Western democracies stand together in strict adherence to the principles of the United Nations Charter, their influence for furthering these principles will be immense and no one is likely to molest them. If, however, they become divided or falter in their duty, and if these all-important years are allowed to slip away, then indeed catastrophe may overwhelm us all.

Last time I saw it all coming and cried aloud to my fellow countrymen and to the world, but no one paid any attention. Up til the year 1933, or even 1935, Germany might have been saved from the awful fate which has overtaken her and we might all have been spared the miseries that Hitler let loose upon mankind. There never was a war in all history easier to prevent by timely action than the one which has just desolated such great areas of the globe. It could have been prevented without the firing of a single shot, and Germany might be powerful, prosperous, and honored today, but no one would listen, and one by one we were all sucked into the awful whirlpool.

We surely must not let that happen again. This can only be achieved by reaching now, in 1946, a good understanding on all points with Russia under the general authority of the United Nations Organization and by the maintenance of that good understanding through many peaceful years, by the world instrument, supported by the whole strength of the English-speaking world and all its connections.

Let no man underrate the abiding power of the British Empire and Commonwealth. Because you see the 46 million in our island harassed about their food supply, of which they grew only one-half, even in wartime, or because we have difficulty in restarting our industries and export trade after six years of passionate war effort, do not suppose that we shall not come through these dark years of privation as we have come through the glorious years of agony, or that half a century from now you will not see 70 or 80 million Britons spread about the world and united in defense of our traditions, our way of life, and of the world causes we and you espouse.

If the population of the English-speaking Commonwealth be added to that of the United States, with all that such cooperation implies in the air, on the sea, and in science and industry, there will be no quivering, precarious balance of power to offer its temptation to ambition or adventure. On the contrary, there will be an overwhelming assurance of security. If we adhere faithfully to the charter of the United Nations and walk forward in sedate and sober strength, seeking no one's land or treasure, or seeking to lay no arbitrary control on the thoughts of men, if all British moral and material forces and convictions are joined with your own in fraternal association, the highroads of the future will be clear, not only for us, but for all, not only for our time, but for a century to come.

HARRY S. TRUMAN: THE TRUMAN DOCTRINE

The gravity of the situation which confronts the world today necessitates my appearance before a joint session of the Congress. The foreign policy and the national security of this country are involved.

One aspect of the present situation which I wish to present to you at this time for your consideration and decision concerns Greece and Turkey. The United States has received from the Greek government an urgent appeal for financial and economic assistance. Preliminary reports from the American economic mission now in Greece and reports from the American ambassador in Greece corroborate the statement of the Greek government that assistance is imperative if Greece is to survive as a free nation.

I do not believe that the American people and the Congress wish to turn a deaf ear to the appeal of the Greek government.

Greece is not a rich country. Lack of sufficient natural resources has always forced the Greek people to work hard to make both ends meet. Since 1940, this industrious and peace-loving country has suffered invasion, four years of cruel enemy occupation, and bitter internal strife.

When forces of liberation entered Greece they found that retreating Germans had destroyed virtually all the railways, roads, port facilities, communications, and merchant marine. More than a thousand villages had been burned. Eighty-five percent of the children were tubucular. Livestock, poultry, and draft animals had almost disappeared. Inflation had wiped out practically all savings. As a result of these tragic conditions, a militant minority, exploiting human want and misery, was able to create political chaos which, until now, has made economic recovery impossible.

Greece is today without funds to finance the importation of those goods which are essential to bare subsistence. Under these circumstances the people of Greece cannot make progress in solving their problems of reconstruction. Greece is in desperate need of financial and economic assistance to enable it to resume purchases of food, clothing, fuel and seeds. These are indispensable for the subsistence of its people and are obtainable only from abroad. Greece must have help to import the goods necessary to restore internal order and security so essential for economic and political recovery.

The Greek government has also asked for the assistance of experienced American administrators, economists, and technicians to insure that the financial and other aid given to Greece shall be used effectively in creating a stable and self-sustaining economy and in improving its public administration.

The very existence of the Greek state is today threatened by the terriorist activities of several thousand armed men, led by Communists, who defy the government's authority at a number of points, particularly along the northern boundaries. A commission appointed by the United Nations Security Council is at present investigating disturbed conditions in northern Greece and alleged border violations along the frontier between Greece, on the one hand, and Albania, Bulgaria, and Yugoslavia, on the other. Meanwhile, the Greek government is unable to cope with the situation. The Greek Army is small and poorly equipped. It needs supplies and equipment if it is to restore the authority of the government throughout Greek territory.

Greece must have assistance if it is to become a self-supporting and self-respecting democracy. The United States must supply this assistance. We have already extended to Greece certain types of relief and economic aid but these are inadequate. There is no other country to which democratic Greece can turn. No other nation is willing to provide the necessary support for a democratic Greek government.

The British government, which has been helping Greece, can give no further financial or economic aid after March 31. Great Britain finds itself under the necessity of liquidating its commitments in several parts of the world, including Greece.

We have considered how the United Nations might assist in this crisis. But the situation is an urgent one requiring immediate action, and the United Nations and its related organizations are not in a position to extend help of the kind that is required.

It is important to note that the Greek government has asked for our aid in utilizing effectively the financial and other assistance we may give to Greece and in improving its public administration. It is of the utmost importance that we supervise the use of any funds made available to Greece in such a manner that each dollar spent will count toward making Greece self-supporting and will help to build an economy in which a healthy democracy can flourish.

No government is perfect. One of the chief virtues of a democracy, however, is that its defects are always visible and under democratic process can be pointed out and corrected. The government of Greece is not perfect. Nevertheless, it represents 35 percent of the members of the Greek Parliament who were chosen in an election last year. Foreign observers, including 692 Americans, considered this election to be a fair expression of the views of the Greek people.

The Greek government has been operating in an atmosphere of chaos and extremism. It has made mistakes. The extension of aid by this country does not mean that the United States condones everything that the Greek government has done or will do. We have condemned in the past, and we will condemn now, extremist measures of the right or the left. We have in the past advised tolerance, and we advise tolerance now.

Greece's neighbor, Turkey, also deserves our attention. The future of Turkey as an independent and economically sound state is clearly no less important to the freedom-loving peoples of the world than the future of Greece. The circumstances in which Turkey finds itself today are considerably different from those of Greece. Turkey has been spared the disasters that have beset Greece. And during the war, the United States and Great Britain furnished Turkey with material aid. Nevertheless, Turkey now needs our support.

Since the war, Turkey has sought financial assistance from Great Britain and the United States for the purpose of effecting that modernization necessary for the maintenance of its national integrity. That integrity is essential to the preservation of order in the Middle East.

The British government has informed us that, owing to its own difficulties, it can no longer extend financial or economic aid to Turkey. As in the case of Greece, if Turkey is to have the assistance it needs, the United States must supply it. We are the only country able to provide that help.

I am fully aware of the broad implications involved if the United States extends assistance to Greece and Turkey and I shall discuss these implications with you at this time.

One of the primary objectives of the foreign policy of the United States is the creation of conditions in which we and other nations will be able to work out a way of life free from coercion. This was a fundamental issue in the way with Germany and Japan. Our victory was won over countries which sought to impose their will and their way of life upon other nations.

To insure the peaceful development of nations, free from coercion, the United States has taken a leading part in establishing the United Nations. The United Nations is designed to make possible lasting freedom and independence for all its members. We shall not realize our objectives, however, unless we are willing to help free people to maintain their free institutions and their national integrity against aggressive movements that seek to impose upon them totalitarian regimes. This is no more than a frank recognition that totalitarian regimes imposed on free peoples, by direct or indirect aggression, undermine the foundation of international peace and hence the security of the United States.

The peoples of a number of countries of the world have recently had totalitarian regimes forced upon them against their will. The government of the United States has made frequent protests against coercion and intimidation, in violation of the Yalta Agreement, in Poland, Rumania, and Bulgaria. I must also state that in a number of other countries there have been similar developments.

At the present moment in world history nearly every nation must choose between alternative ways of life. The choice is too often not a free one.

One way of life is based upon the will of the majority, and is distinguished by free institutions, representative government, free elections, guarantees of individual liberty, freedom of speech and religion, and freedom from political oppression. The second way of life is based upon the will of a minority forcibly imposed upon the majority. It relies on terror and oppression, a controlled press and radio, fixed elections, and the suppression of personal freedom.

I believe that it must be the policy of the United States to support free peoples who are resisting attempted subjugation by armed minorities or by outside pressures. I believe that we must assist free peoples to work out their own destinies in their own way. I believe that our help should be primarily through economic and financail aid, which is essential to economic stability and orderly political process.

The world is not static and the status quo is not sacred. But we cannot allow changes in the status quo in violation of the Charter of the United Nations by such methods as coercion or by such subterfuge as political infiltration. In helping free and independent nations to maintain their freedom, the United States will be giving effect to the principles of the Charter of the United Nations.

It is necessary only to glance at a map to realize that the survival and integrity of the Greek nation are of grave importance in a much wider situation. If Greece should fall under the control of an armed minority, the effect upon its neighbor, Turkey, would be immediate and serious. Confusion and disorder might well spread throughout the entire Middle East. Moreover, the disappearance of Greece as an independent state would have a profound effect upon those countries in Europe whose people are struggling against great difficulties to maintain their freedoms and their independence while they repair the damages of war.

It would be an unspeakable tragedy if these countries, which have struggled so long against overwhelming odds, should lose that victory for which they sacrificed so much. Collapse of free institutions and loss of independence would be disastrous not only for them but for the world. Discouragement and possibly failure would quickly be the lot of neighboring peoples striving to maintain their freedom and independence.

Should we fail to aid Greece and Turkey in this fateful hour, the effect will be far-reaching to the West as well as to the East. We must take immediate and resolute action.

I therefore ask Congress to provide authority for assistance to Greece and Turkey in the amount of $400 million for the period ending June 30, 1948. In requesting these funds, I have taken into consideration the maximum amount of relief assistance which would be furnished to Greece out of the $350 million which I recently requested that the Congress authorize for the prevention of starvation and suffering in countries devastated by the war.

In addition to funds, I ask Congress to authorize the detail of American civilian and military personnel to Greece and Turkey, at the request of those countries, to assist in the tasks of reconstruction, and for the purpose of supervising the use of such financial and material assistance as may be furnished. I recommend that authority also be provided for the instruction and training of selected Greek and Turkish personnel.

Finally, I ask that the Congress provide the authority which will permit the speediest and most effective use, in terms of needed commodities, supplies and equipment, of such funds as may be authorized.

If further funds, or further authority should be needed for purposes indicated in this message, I shall not hesitate to bring the situation before the Congress. On this subject the executive and legislative branches of the government must work together.

This is a serious course upon which we embark. I would not recommend it except that the alternative is much more serious.

The United States contributed $341 billion toward winning World War II. This is an investment in world freedom and world peace. The assistance that I am recommending for Greece and Turkey amounts to little more than one-tenth of 1 percent of this investment. It is only common sense that we should safeguard this investment and make sure that it was not in vain.

The seeds of totalitarian regimes are nurtured by misery and want. They spread and grow in the evil soil of poverty and strife. They reach their full growth when the hope of a people for a better life has died. We must keep that hope alive.

The free peoples of the world look to us for support in maintaining their freedoms. If we falter in our leadership, we may endanger the peace of the world—and we shall surely endanger the welfare of our own nation.

Great responsibilities have been placed upon us by the swift movement of events. I am confident that Congress will face these responsibilities squarely.

GEORGE C. MARSHALL: THE MARSHALL PLAN

I need not tell you gentlemen that the world situation is very serious. That must be apparent to all intelligent people. I think one difficulty is that the problem is one of such enormous complexity that the very mass of facts presented to the publics by press and radio make it exceedingly difficult for the man in the street to reach a clear appraisement of the situation. Furthermore, the people of this country are distant from the troubled area of the earth and it is hard for them to comprehend the plight and consequent reactions of the long-suffering peoples, and the effect of those reactions of their governments in connection with our efforts to promote peace in the world.

In considering the requirements for the rehabilitation of Europe, the physical loss of life, the visible destruction of cities, factories, mines, and railroads was correctly estimated; but it has become obvious during recent months that this visible destruction was probably less serious than the dislocation of the entire fabric of European economy. For the past ten years conditions have been highly abnormal. The feverish preparation for war and the more feverish maintenance of the war effort engulfed all aspects of national economies. Machinery has fallen into disrepair or is entirely obsolete. Under the arbitrary and destructive Nazi rule, virtually every possible enterprise was geared into the German war machine. Long-standing commercial ties, private institutions, banks, insurance companies, and shipping companies disappeared through loss of capital, absorption through nationalization, or by simple destruction. In many countries, confidence in the local currency has been severely shaken.

The breakdown of the business structure of Europe during the war was complete. Recovery has been seriously retarded by the fact that two years after the close of hostilities a peace settlement with Germany and Austria has not been agreed upon. But even given a more prompt solution of these difficult problems, the rehabilitation of the economic structure of Europe quite evidently will require a much longer time and greater effort than had been foreseen.

There is a phase of this matter which is both interesting and serious. The farmer has always produced the foodstuffs to exchange with the city dweller for the other necessities of life. This division of labor is the basis of modern civilization. At the present time it is threatened with breakdown. The town and city industries are not producing adequate goods to exchange with the food-producing farmer. Raw materials and fuel are in short supply. Machinery is lacking or worn out. The farmer or the peasant cannot find the goods for sale which he desires to purchase. So the sale of his farm produce for money which he cannot use seems to him an unprofitable transaction. He, therefore, has withdrawn many fields from crop cultivation and is using them for grazing. He feeds more grain to stock and finds for himself and his family an ample supply of food, however short he may be on clothing and the other ordinary gadgets of civilization.

Meanwhile people in the cities are short of food and fuel. So the governments are forced to use their foreign money and credits to procure these necessities abroad. This process exhausts funds which are urgently needed for reconstruction. Thus a very serious situation is rapidly developing which bodes no good for the world. The modern system of the division of labor upon which the exchange of products is based is in danger of breaking down.

The truth of the matter is that Europe's requirements for the next three or four years of foreign food and other essential products—principally from America—are so much greater than her present ability to pay that she must have substantial additional help or face economic, social, and political deterioration of a very grave character.

The remedy lies in breaking the vicious circle and restoring the confidence of the European people in the economic future of their own countries and of Europe as a whole. The manufacturer and the farmer throughout wide areas must be able and willing to exchange their products for currencies the continuing value of which is not open to question.

Aside from the demoralizing effect on the world at large and the possibilities of disturbances arising as a result of the desperation of the people concerned, the consequences to the economy of the United States should be apparent to all. It is logical that the United States should do whatever it is able to do to assist in the return of normal economic health in the world, without which there can be no political stability and no assured peace. Our policy is directed not against any country or doctrine but against hunger, poverty, desperation, and chaos. Its purpose should be the revival of a working economy in the world so as to permit the emergence of political and social conditions in which free institutions can exist.

Such assistance, I am convinced, must not be on a piecemeal basis as various crises develop. Any assistance that this government may render in the future should provide a cure rather than a mere palliative. Any government that is willing to assist in the task of recovery will find full cooperation, I am sure, on the part of the United States government. Any government which maneuvers to block the recovery cannot expect help from us. Furthermore, governments, political parties or groups which seek to perpetuate human misery in order to profit therefrom politically or otherwise will encounter the opposition of the United States.

It is already evident that, before the United States government can proceed much further in its efforts to alleviate the situation and help start the European world on its way to recovery, there must be some agreement among the countries of Europe as to the requirements of the situation and the part those countries themselves will take in order to give proper effect to whatever actions might be undertaken by this government. It would be neither fitting nor efficacious for this government to undertake to draw up unilaterally a program designed to place Europe on it feet economically. This is the business of the Europeans. The initiative, I think, must come from Europe. The role of this country should consist of friendly aid in the drafting of a European program and of later support of such a program so far as it may be practical for us to do so. The program should be a joint one, agreed to by a number of, if not all, European nations. An essential part of any successful action on the part of the United States is an understanding on the part of the people of America of the character of the problem and the remedies to be applied. Political passion and prejudice should have no part. With foresight, and a willingness on the part of our people to face up to the vast responsibility which history has clearly placed upon our country, the difficulties I have outlined can and will be overcome.

GLOSSARY

allies the countries with which America cooperates most closely. Examples would be England, France, Japan, and West Germany.

"balance of power" system a joining together of countries in international relations so that each group of countries feels protected from its enemies. One alliance balances another alliance.

bipolar the division of the world after World War II into two parts, or poles, the American side and the Soviet side.

checks and balances the system of government where political power is broken up or shared among several actors. The separation of powers in the U.S. Constitution guarantees these checks and balances. This system is the opposite of centralized power.

Cold War the hostile relationship that developed in the late 1940s between the Soviet Union and the nations of the West, mainly the United States. The Cuban Missile Crisis marked the end of the Cold War.

collective security the idea that all nations unite to act with the same purpose. This was Woodrow Wilson's suggestion about how to overcome the problems of the balance of power system. The League of Nations and the United Nations are both examples of the idea of collective security.

commercial relations relations or interactions with other countries that involve "commerce." Commercial relations can also be called business or economic relations.

consensus agreement. If there is a national consensus on foreign policy, most people agree that they support the policy.

containment the American policy, developed by George Kennan after World War I, of being very firm with the Soviets to prevent them from expanding their influence in the world.

detente the policy of a relaxation in tensions between the two superpowers. It started in the early 1960s, replacing the Cold War attitude.

domestic policy the programs which a country has within the country. Examples would be policies on housing, social security, farming, or health insurance.

domino theory the idea that if one country falls to Communism, then others will follow. This theory was often used to explain America's defense of Vietnam.

foreign policy the programs which a country has toward other countries. Examples would be policies on national security, economics and trade, relations with poor countries, or international refugees.

founding fathers the men who wrote the Constitution and decided what kind of government America should have.

Fourteen Points Woodrow Wilson's specific suggestions for a peace plan at the end of World War I. The president had to compromise on most of his points, and the U.S. Senate rejected the peace treaty.

idealist-liberal view the vision of U.S. involvement in the world that focuses on longer-term global problems such as ignorance, poverty, and pollution. The Soviet threat is only of secondary importance.

interdependence the linkage of countries in the world due to similar factors and problems. Countries cannot solve problems concerning drugs, food, outer space, pollution, and other areas without cooperation. Interdependence signals a shift from a bipolar to a multipolar world.

Iron Curtain Churchill's famous description of the border between democratic Western Europe and Communist Eastern Europe.

isolationism the policy of depending only on oneself. America wanted to remain separate from Europe and the politics of the Old World in the nineteenth century. Some Americans still tend to favor a policy of isolationism today, but it has become almost impossible due to the close links between all countries.

League of Nations Woodrow Wilson's main idea on how to avoid future world wars. All nations would work *collectively* ("collective security") to prevent any future wars. The United Nations represented a similar idea at the end of World War II.

Marshall Plan the massive $13 billion program financed by the United States for the recover of Western Europe after World War II.

Monroe Doctrine the basic principle of American foreign policy throughout the nineteenth century. The United States declared that it would protect other countries in the Western Hemisphere from foreign domination.

moralism the American tradition of feeling that we can and should serve as a model to other countries. Woodrow Wilson and Jimmy Carter both emphasized moralism.

National Security Act of 1947 the law passed by Congress in 1947 to give the president a stronger role in making foreign policy. It expanded the Department of State and created the Department of Defense, the Central Intelligence Agency, and the National Security Council.

national security adviser the president's chief foreign policy adviser *within* the White House. The adviser is head of the National Security Council, and he sees the president more than any other foreign policy expert.

North Atlantic Treaty Organization (NATO) the alliance formed in 1949 between several Western European and North American countries for the military defense of the Western world.

Old World the European countries. The settlers who left Europe for North America called their new home the "New World."

realist-conservative view the vision of American involvement in the world that focuses on using American military strength to contain the Soviet threat.

Rough Riders the name of Theodore Roosevelt's unit in the Spanish-American War. Individual units of volunteers, rather than the American army, fought the war.

secretary of state the chief foreign policy-maker in the executive branch. The secretary of state is in charge of the State Department and its thousands of employees.

separation of powers the idea in the U.S. Constitution to divide power or responsibility in government among the executive, legislative, and judicial branches. The advantage is that no one branch has too much power. The disadvantage is that policy decisions are more difficult.

Spanish-American War the war with Spain in 1898, supposedly fought over Spain's role in Cuba. The war also demonstrated clearly that the United States was a world power.

Truman Doctrine this completely new U.S. foreign policy, introduced in 1947, put emphasis on economic assistance as a response to the dangers of Communist totalitarianism. The Marshall Plan was a direct result of the Truman Doctrine.

Washington's Farewell Address the speech given by George Washington as he finished his second term as president. He warned the United States to avoid involvement with the politics of Europe.

BIBLIOGRAPHY

Articles

Every day in the newspapers, and every week and month in a variety of magazines, there are relevant articles on foreign policy and foreign affairs. A small number of articles is provided below:

"A Contra Aid Plan," *Newsweek*, October 13,1986,

Carter, J. "Middle East: Time for Negotiations," *Time*, April 20, 1987,

Church, G.J. "Now, Super-Zero?" *Time*, April 27, 1987,

Kegley, C.W., and Wittkopf, E.R. "The Two Faces of the Reagan Administration's Foreign Policy Approach," *USA Today*, January 1987,

Lamar, J.V. "The Missiles of Europe," *Time*, October 13, 1986,

"NATO: Changes Ahead," *Newsweek*, December 1, 1986,

"A Poll: Europe vs. the U.S." *Newsweek*, April 28, 1986,

Range, P.R. "Probing for an Africa Policy," *U.S. News and World Report*, January 19, 1987,

Smolowe, J. "Pacific Overtures," *Time*, November 17, 1986,

"The Iran Coverup [Special Section]", *Newsweek*, March 2, 1987,

Books

World War II to the present

Acheson, Dean. *Present at the Creation: My Years at the State Department*. New York: W.W. Norton, 1969.

Ambrose, Stephen E. *Eisenhower Vol. II: The President*. New York: Simon and Schuster, 1984.

Ball, George W. *Diplomacy for a Crowded World*. Boston: Little, Brown, 1976.

Brewer, Thomas L. *American Foreign Policy: A Contemporary Introduction*. Englewood Clifts, N.J.: Prentice-Hall, 1986.

Combs, Jerald A. *The History of American Foreign Policy*. New York: Alfred A. Knopf, 1986.

Crabb, Cecil V., Jr., and Mulcahy, Kevin V. *Presidents and Foreign Policy Making: From FDR to Reagan*. La.: Louisiana State University Press, 1986.

Craig, Gordon A., and George, Alexander L. *Force and Statecraft*. New York: Oxford University Press, 1983.

Deibel, Terry L., and Gaddis, John Lewis, eds.. *Containment: Concept and Policy*. Washington, D.C.: National Defense University Press, 1986.

Denny, Brewster C. *Seeing American Foreign Policy Whole*. Chicago: University of Illinois Press, 1985.

Dougherty, James E., and Pfatzgraff, Robert L., Jr. *American Foreign Policy: FDR to Reagan*. New York: Harper and Row, 1986.

Faringdon, Hugh. *Confrontation: The Strategic Geography of NATO and the Warsaw Pact*. Methuen, 1986.

Gaddis, John Lewis. *Strategies of Containment*. New York: Oxford University Press, 1982.

Hersh, Seymour M. *The Price of Power*. New York: Summit Books, 1983.

Hill, Kenneth L. *Concise Overview of Foreign Policy*, Krieger, 1986.

Joint Working Group of the Atlantic Council of the U.S., and the Citizens Network for Foreign Affairs. *U.S. International Leadership for the 21st Century: Building a National Foreign Affairs Constituency*. Washington D.C.: Joint Working Group of the Atlantic Council of the U.S., and the Citizens Network for Foreign Affairs, 1987.

Kalb, Marvin, and Kalb, Bernard. *Kissinger*. Boston: Little, Brown, 1979.

Kearns, Doris. *Lyndon Johnson and the American Dream*. New York: Harper and Row, 1976.

Kennedy, Robert F. *Thirteen Days*. New York: W.W. Norton, 1969.

Kimball, Warren F. *Franklin D. Roosevelt and the World Crisis, 1937–1945*. Lexington, Mass.: D.C. Heath, 1973.

Oye, Kenneth A.; Lieber, Robert J. and Rothchild, Donald, eds. *Eagle Resurgent? The Reagan Era in American Foreign Policy*. Boston: Little, Brown, 1986.

Quester, George H. *American Foreign Policy*. New York: Praeger Publishers, 1982.

Reilly, John E., ed. *American Public Opinion and U.S. Foreign Policy 1987*. Chicago: The Chicago Council on Foreign Relations, 1987.

Sabrosky, Alan N. *Alliances in U.S. Foreign Policy: NATO and the Quest for Collective Defense*. Westview, 1986.

Schlesinger, Arthur M., Jr. *A Thousand Days: John F. Kennedy in the White House*. Boston: Houghton Miffin, 1965.

Schloming, Gordon C. *American Foreign Policy and the Nuclear Dilemma*. Englewood Cliffs, N.J.: Prentice-Hall, 1987.

Serfaty, Simon. *American Foreign Policy in a Hostile World: Dangerous Years*. New York: Praeger Publishers, 1984.

Sidey, Hugh. *John F. Kennedy, President*. New York: Fawcett, 1963.

Spainer, John. *American Foreign Policy Since World War II*. 8th ed. New York: Holt, Rhinehart, and Winston, 1980.

Tuchman, Barbara. *Stilwell and the American Experience in China*. New York: Macmillan, 1970.

Wilson, James Q. *American Government*. Lexington, Mass. D.C. Heath, 1980.

Diplomatic History 1776–1933

Bemis, Samuel Flagg. *John Quincy Adams and the Foundation of American Foreign Policy*. New York: W.W. Norton, 1973.

Burton, David H. *Theodore Roosevelt: Confident Imperialist*. Philadelphia: University of Pennsylvania Press, 1968.

Dulles, Foster Rhea. *America's Rise to World Power, 1898–1954*. New York: Harper and Row, 1963.

Kennan, George F. *American Foreign Policy, 1900–1954*. Chicago: Chicago University Press, 1951.

May, Ernest R. *The World War and American Isolationism, 1914–1917*. Chicago: Quadrangle, 1959.

Perkins, Dexter. *The Monroe Doctrine, 1823–1826*. Cambridge, Mass.: Harvard University Press, 1927.

Varg, Paul. *Foreign Policies of the Founding Fathers*. East Lansing, Mich.: Michigan State University Press, 1963.

INDEX